Let Me Down

Let Me Down

REFLECTIONS ON ABUSE AND LOVE

CALLIE RAE O'REILLY

ECW

Published by ECW Press
665 Gerrard Street East
Toronto, Ontario, Canada M4M 1Y2
416-694-3348 / info@ecwpress.com

CERTIFIED CANADIAN PUBLISHER

Editor for the Press: Pia Singhal
Copy editor: Megan Beadle
Cover design: Caroline Suzuki
Cover artwork: "Dove Flying Out of a Bird Cage" (c) CSA-Printstock / iStock

To the best of her abilities, the author has related experiences, places, people, and organizations from her memories of them. In order to protect the privacy of others, she has, in some instances, changed the names of certain people and details of events and places.

LIBRARY AND ARCHIVES CANADA CATALOGUING IN PUBLICATION

Title: Let me down : reflections on abuse and love / Callie Rae O'Reilly.

Names: O'Reilly, Callie Rae, author.

Identifiers: Canadiana (print) 20260118516 | Canadiana (ebook) 20260118583

ISBN 978-1-77041-848-6 (softcover)
ISBN 978-1-77852-564-3 (PDF)
ISBN 978-1-77852-563-6 (ePub)

Subjects: LCSH: O'Reilly, Callie Rae. | LCSH: Abused women—Canada—Biography. | LCSH: Intimate partner violence—Canada. | LCGFT: Autobiographies.

Classification: LCC HV6626.23.C3 O75 2026 | DDC 362.82/92092—dc23

This book is funded in part by the Government of Canada. *Ce livre est financé en partie par le gouvernement du Canada.* We acknowledge the support of the Canada Council for the Arts. *Nous remercions le Conseil des arts du Canada de son soutien.* We would like to acknowledge the funding support of the Ontario Arts Council (OAC) and the Government of Ontario for their support. We also acknowledge the support of the Government of Ontario through the Ontario Book Publishing Tax Credit, and through Ontario Creates.

Canada

Canada Council for the Arts
Conseil des arts du Canada

Ontario

ONTARIO ARTS COUNCIL
CONSEIL DES ARTS DE L'ONTARIO
an Ontario government agency
un organisme du gouvernement de l'Ontario

ONTARIO CREATES

PRINTED AND BOUND IN CANADA

PRINTING: MARQUIS 5 4 3 2 1

For my family.

This book discusses physical and sexual abuse,
amongst other things.

Please take care of yourself while reading.

Some names and details have been changed.

AUTHOR'S NOTE

I never thought a boyfriend of mine would hit me.

I was too smart for that.

I would be different, see the glaring signs and walk out the door.

But abuse moves like a slow-motion trap, and at nineteen, I didn't understand this. I also believed my lack of black eyes and sickening adoration for him made my situation somehow different, especially when so much of the abuse was disguised as sex and quickly became my own shame.

In the decade since, I began to look back at it all with different eyes. Adult eyes. It wasn't until years passed that I could see how much had really happened to me, while simultaneously realizing the world isn't a safe place for victims who share (something sharply highlighted by the recent treatment of Amber Heard). Seems it's easier to dismiss a woman's experience than face the reality of violent men. But we know things only evolve when dragged out of the shadows.

So, here is my best retelling of an experience, complicated and common but less often told. I'm embarrassed by a lot of it — most of it, really — but I don't want to be. Instead, I've gone back in time to my messiest days, dusted off journals and memories I wish I didn't have, and did my best to accurately lay them out here for you, for all victims, to hopefully begin to unburden ourselves.

My goal isn't to vilify or open old wounds. It's to talk, to tell, to articulate and assign language, especially for the sake of women younger than me. Because abuse is confusing. Blinding. And we aren't warned the way we need to be.

I spent years grappling with self-blame and doubting my own memories, which plagued my dreams. And honestly, I don't really know why. I could attribute it to the societal tolerance of violent men or the effects of trauma. Both, I know, are factors. But really, I think it's because I am still surprised, to this day, that this happened to me.

PROLOGUE

Although I told myself I could handle it, I knew early on I was in over my head.

We'd been seeing each other for two years, but the electricity between us hadn't waned no matter how many months ticked by. Reed was experienced, but for me, everything was a thrilling first. His enthusiasm was exhilarating and my lack of experience seemed to be exactly what thrilled him.

Our sex life had evolved. He used to be gentle. I'd never experienced the progression of a long-term relationship, leaving me with no knowledge of what was considered "normal." I didn't know how our personal life compared to those of my friends or if most relationships revolved almost entirely around sex, the way ours did. But inside, I had my suspicions Reed was rougher than most. This became increasingly clear when I occasionally shared a tidbit or two with girlfriends who looked back at me wide-eyed and said something like, "Wow . . . well good for you guys." My stomach tightened.

The truth was, Reed scared me. What my friends didn't know was that I'd been slapped across the face and choked, both in bed and in my front hallway, while his eyes were black with anger. Deep into the world Reed and I had cultivated, my blinders fastened so tight, the line between the violence in our relationship and what I perceived to be the maturity of our sexual relationship was unrecognizable. I couldn't see through the haziness of dual demonstrations of both passion and rage, of an adult sex life and domestic violence. My young mind was drowning.

My excuses swore there must be a disconnect happening for Reed. I felt that perhaps he didn't see the difference between being violent with me during an argument and the way some people consensually choose to have sex. I thought maybe, based on his own life's baggage and whatever trauma he experienced — or simply his personal preference — we were seeing these two parts of our relationship differently.

And yet, I started to develop a taste for the deep entanglements that came with these lines of consent being blurred and began to see twisted value in it. We were carrying with us such complication and nuance only the two of us could understand. As we became more complicated and our world drifted further away from everything we knew, I accepted the lurking monster. Everything I thought I knew about connection and intimacy was flipped on its head and I could no longer remember the beliefs I held about men before Reed. To make matters even more confusing, I wasn't sure I wanted to remember.

Reed ushered us into a place entirely of our own, where his aggression was normal. I liked being able to handle someone as experienced and enigmatic as him. It made me feel special. So did keeping a secret. Reed's outbursts also assured me he cared, as he rarely made it clear in healthier ways. I wanted this older man I was in love with to be himself with me. I wanted him to get the things he wanted from *me*, for us to share a connection different from how I imagined other couples' relationships looked, in healthy ways or not.

Eventually, Reed and I decided to film ourselves having sex. The toughest part for me to admit is that I think it was my idea. I hoped it might keep me interesting, and my days were easier when he was happy. But as soon as the words came out of my mouth, I heard the smallest, most faint echo of pre-emptive shame whispering from the deepest corner of my gut. Undetectable to untrained ears, but I heard it.

We agreed we would watch it once, then delete it forever.

I joked with him, "If you ever do anything with it, I will just die!"

He assured me, "I'm in it, too. Why would I want anyone to see it?"

I nodded. It was my idea, after all. I couldn't change my mind. He wouldn't like that. I did my best to believe his reassurances, but my gut tapped me on the shoulder, reminding me of the hole in my door, his hands around my throat, the reasons not to trust him.

As our relationship carried on, the weight of our blurred lines followed us closely, no matter how much we tried to zig and zag. Like a bitter aftertaste I couldn't rinse out. As we sat, legs intertwined, tucked in a downtown bar, I felt it written all over my face. I worried what I'd say after one vodka soda too many. Or even sober. When I laughed with my hand on his warm chest or ran my hands over his collarbones, my body flashed to being thrown down onto my bed, his hand covering my mouth. My body was always eager to remind me of our dirty secret and how it had bled into our sex life. Or maybe out of it. It didn't matter how much he made my friends laugh or the way I loved his smile, there was black mould.

Once we filmed the video, I don't remember hearing much about it at all. We never talked about it. It wasn't that we were avoiding the topic, it just never came up. I'd seen bits and pieces, just enough to know I wasn't interested in ever seeing more. It was slightly mortifying, but I wrote it off as something fun we did together. I was proud of myself for trying something so wildly outside of my parameters. Isn't this what your early adult years are all about? It would be months before the tape reared its head again, and by that time, our relationship was unrecognizable.

MEETING

CHAPTER 1

I first saw Reed while the summer heat still lingered in the afternoons. It was autumn, and as a fresh university student, my mental health was the worst it had ever been. My anxiety was entirely out of control and now it had company as depression entered my brain and made itself comfortable. I'd never struggled with self-esteem issues before this, I wasn't equipped to handle the growing list of insecurities with my body. I didn't know how to help myself when just getting out of bed in the morning took more willpower than I had on reserve.

Born and raised in Toronto before moving north at fourteen, I planned to move to the States for university. But when my mental health deteriorated suddenly toward the end of high school, moving that far from home wasn't possible. Instead, I enrolled at a school closer to home and swapped the yellow cabs of New York for the red streetcars of Toronto. It was an art school, just two hours away from my parents, so on my worst days, I could retreat.

We met at the corner bar on our shared block, thanks to my older sister's ID. I was a graphic design student, he was an aspiring photographer. One shy glance was enough; I fell in love with him right then and there. His thick hair was jet-black, and, it seemed, intentionally messy — the kind boys have on screen and yet curiously never seem to have in real life. His features were dramatic: piercing green eyes, dark, low eyebrows and a small gap between his front teeth. He was quiet but confident, offering just the bare minimum. I'd heard about these types of men — the ones who are so withholding, you find yourself craving any piece of them — but I'd never met one.

I stood next to him, both of us leaning against the back wall of the bar.

"So what do you photograph?" I asked, not knowing where else to start.

With a shrug and a hint of a smile, his eyes turned warm. "Mostly portraits."

He was going to make me work for it. Eyeing tattoos poking out from under his long sleeve, I was equal parts intimidated and fascinated. I was a baby, not long out of high school, clawing at the door of my twenties. But he was twenty-four. He was also shiny and new. There were no dark-haired, creative, aloof boys in my small-town high school.

The summer before grade nine, my parents sold our house in Toronto and moved us to 70 acres on a dirt road. It was jarring, no matter how much warning we'd been given. For elementary school, I had been at a Toronto public school with eight hundred kids. High school looked a bit different at a tennis camp turned private school with just 150 students, nestled near the base of a ski mountain. I wore a navy-blue sweater vest, grey kilt, and knee socks. The school went all the way from kindergarten through grade twelve and there were just under twenty kids in my grade. But lucky for me, Aidan was one of them. We met when we were fourteen, and at sixteen, we started dating.

There's nothing quite like the butterflies, heart-racing, giddy excitement of a new crush. That fleeting time just after meeting someone new when your imagination can run shamelessly wild. Aidan was funny and loud — the class clown — who could be mesmerizing to some and intimidating to others. He relished making you squirm. We had a solid, surprisingly mature relationship for teenagers. He was forthcoming with his feelings, telling me he loved me a few months into dating, and after that, never going a day without making me feel like the only girl in the room. With Aidan came a very specific joy, always making teachers laugh as he talked himself out of an assignment or missed a deadline or looked for the next opportunity to entertain the class.

I spent most cold, blustery Saturday nights not at parties or with friends, but at the local arena watching Aidan play hockey. After the game, I'd wait for him outside of the locker room with the other girlfriends. They were the pretty girls: the cheerleaders with clear skin, blonde hair, and just the right wash of jeans. I'd sit alone on a bench across the room. Being from the small school in town, I didn't know anyone. The boys would trickle out, playing it cool and greeting their girlfriends with side-hugs. Ever social, Aidan was usually one of the last to emerge, but I wouldn't get a cool-guy hug like the others. Instead, he'd pretend to take me out from behind the knee with a hockey stick or press a sweaty hockey glove over my nose for a quick second. Laughing at his own joke, he'd throw an arm around my shoulders, hair still dripping from the shower, and say, "Let's get outta here." As he constantly teased me, there was a simplicity to the way I loved Aidan and Aidan loved me. Not yet jaded by heartbreak, we existed only for each other, living for each Monday morning when we had the house to ourselves and spending our nights on the phone, promising to one day be married. He was every parent's dream for their daughter's first boyfriend. Considerate and gentle, funny and protective. Aidan laid the groundwork for how I believed being a girlfriend would always feel: special, important, yet, occasionally antsy.

Aidan and I were different people, and for that reason, we knew we'd eventually reach a crossroads. I was from the city and the city was where I believed I'd end up. Aidan was born and raised in this small town, and even stepping foot into Toronto made him feel like an alien, let alone Manhattan. He didn't like the pace or understand the draw of traffic and restaurant reservations. So just before leaving the bubble of our small town and the safety of Aidan, I decided to end our relationship. We were eighteen, and as adulthood crept closer, the itch to be someone else's girlfriend, to hold a new hand, grew stronger. Even through the thick haze of anxiety, I wanted a bigger bite of independence.

One warm night, we stood leaning against my car, and to the soundtrack of chirping crickets, I ended it.

"We aren't working anymore. You feel it, too. I know it. I can tell." I searched for the words. "You didn't tell me when you had that day off. That would have never happened before."

Aidan's voice turned detached. "Hey, you're the one breaking up with me, not the other way around," he told me. "Don't throw this back at me."

I looked up at him, nausea of pre-emptive regret swirling.

"You can't change your mind this time. If you want to break up, we're breaking up," Aidan told me. I'd tried this a couple times before but was stopped by ice-cold feet.

"I know. I'm sorry."

"Okay, well. That's that, I guess. I'm not doing this again." There was no love left behind his eyes. I'd pushed him too far.

Just a few weeks later, I packed up my bedroom and drove two hours south to the city. My anxiety was so consuming in high school that I never drank. Throughout the peak, it took all my strength just to control the attacks, leaving alcohol out of the question. But this was my new life. I was single and living downtown, had a new group of friends, and now, there was a green-eyed boy.

That night, Reed and I left the bar at the same time, along with my roommate, Marley. I knew Marley from high school. We hadn't been very close, the type of friends who got along well in a group but left alone would quickly run out of things to say, but we decided to be roommates so there'd be at least one familiar face. Marley was gentle yet confident but didn't like to ruffle feathers. She wore lace dresses, floral boots, and braided beads into her hair. I was cynical for my age and my clothes were mostly black. Marley and I were yin and yang, Lennon and McCartney.

"Do you live close by?" I asked Reed, hoping the answer was yes. The bar was just a few doors down from me and Marley's new apartment.

Reed walked with his hands in his jean pockets, eyes mostly glued to the ground, with only a hint of a smirk at the very edge of his mouth when I spoke to him.

"I live just around the corner," he said, nodding his head to the right.

"Do you go to the bar often then?" Marley asked. I knew she was fishing on my behalf.

"Yep." He looked at me. "Too much."

The three of us walked the block slowly while Reed did his best to hold back a smile. Marley and I were both in mini dresses we'd bought back home, he was in jeans and a striped shirt. I was dying to change.

The bubbly excitement of a night out seemed beneath him and I felt his shyness leak into me. Next to Reed, I felt average. He was withdrawn and complicated; I was wide-eyed. Him, mysterious, me, fidgety and naive. Based exclusively on his distance, I decided he would never be interested in me. I was too young, too much of a departure from who he was. Nothing more than a moth fluttering around the eyes of a panther.

My crush only gained momentum as I sunk into my new life free from kilts and curfews. I occasionally ran into him on the street while I walked my puppy, Dexter, sometimes pretending I was too caught up in my headphones to notice. I did my best to look effortlessly cool each time I left my apartment — both he and I shared a love of headphones stretched over a beanie — my eyes scanned the sidewalk for his ratty band T-shirts. A party night at the corner bar without Reed was nothing more than a wasted outfit. Not long after, too nervous and scared of rejection to do it myself, I made Marley sneak up the fire escape and leave a pink Post-It on his door with our phone numbers. Marley didn't mind, but she warned me, "You know, he might start to think it's me that likes him." A duty to pull him out of his shell had taken us both over.

But for weeks, nothing came of it. Reed constantly left his front door propped open. Every day as I walked home from class, my eyes would wander to the top of the fire escape, checking to see whether his door was propped open, and if any lights were on.

Then one night, I lay in bed absent-mindedly flipping through Facebook when my phone lit up.

"Oh, my God." I sat up, clutching my BlackBerry.

"What?" Marley yelled from the next room.

"Reed just texted me, *Do you wanna watch a movie*."

"Really?" Marley slid through my doorway in socks and an oversize T-shirt, smile as big as mine. "And you thought he never noticed you!"

"Wait, but I can't go over there. That's way too scary." It suddenly felt like the last thing I wanted.

"What are you talking about? Of course you're going. You've had your eye on that guy for weeks. Go!"

I thought he barely knew my name. Through his eyes I was young and faceless, not someone to want in bed. That fear was solidified the day I saw him walking into his apartment next to a beautiful girl with the longest legs I'd ever seen. But that night, for whatever reason, he texted me. Maybe he sensed my stomach flutters. Maybe he was just lonely. Whatever the reason, it would change me forever.

I took out my retainer and threw on a better tank top.

"You're not going to wear those sweats, are you?" Marley leaned against the bathroom door frame. Toothbrush between my teeth, I looked down at the grey drawstring pants I'd bought when I was sixteen.

"I was going to . . . Why?"

"Not the hottest outfit I've ever seen. But you do you!"

I shrugged, and a few minutes later said, "Okay, wish me luck."

"Good luck. It'll be fine. Fun, even!"

Excited and petrified, I tiptoed down the hall and out my building's front door, swallowing butterflies. As always, around the corner at the top of the fire escape, Reed's door was propped open an inch. I climbed the rusty stairs and knocked lightly. After a few short seconds, Reed appeared at the door in sock feet, gym shorts, and a distressed Frank Zappa T-shirt.

"Hey."

"Hey." I followed him through the door, past a small, messy living room and into an even smaller bedroom. Reed returned to the floor where he'd been working on his laptop. Reed's bedroom confirmed everything I already believed about who he was. The room was almost completely dark, lit only by the white light of his laptop screen and a couple candles. The curtains were closed and incense burned.

As my eyes adjusted to the near complete darkness of his bedroom, I noticed the walls were full of hanging photographs. "Wow," I said, squinting, examining the walls. "These are beautiful." I assumed they were, anyway.

Without turning to face me, he said, "I don't know." He paused. "Mindless vomit."

His reply was short, strange, and probably didn't reflect how many of his wheels were really turning. I sat down on his nicely-made bed and for a few minutes, he continued to work as if I wasn't there, as if he hadn't just invited me over. I sat watching him, unsure what to do with my hands, wondering if I should keep talking or if he wanted quiet. I glanced at my texts, put my phone down, and picked it back up again. I looked around his room, memorizing every detail to relay to Marley later. Everything was unique: the darkness, the calm, the knick-knacks. Rolls of film and various lenses lined the windowsill. With his back still to me, Reed asked, "So, what do you wanna watch? What are you in the mood for?"

I sighed, "Let me think."

"I just downloaded this Jim Morrison documentary that I've been wanting to watch. Does that interest you?"

It did.

Reed angled his laptop screen just right, pressed play and joined me on the bed. We lay down and he wrapped an arm around my waist. I felt his body press against mine. The year before, this would have taken months to build up to — weeks of quick touches and hesitations. All it took was one text and he was beside me. He seemed confident. A man. I could barely concentrate on the movie, much more interested in feeling his chest move up and down with each breath and the way his wrists were smaller than I expected.

The simplicity of Aidan and me faded in the rearview mirror.

I snuck out before the sun had fully risen, mind already racing. I knew one thing: Reed was experienced and I was not. That much had been brutally obvious.

Shrouded in mystery, sex was only just becoming part of my life. At that age, although my girlfriends and I talked about it, our late-night sharing rarely went deeper than whether or not two people did, in fact, have sex. I wish it had. Hearing other women's experiences could have armed me with knowledge and context.

The first time I slept with Reed was my first time having sex. It's something I never told him, or anyone, but I can't imagine he didn't know — how could he not? I was 6 years younger than Reed, and that night, my greenness shone. I had many experiences with Aidan — experiences we thought were "sex" but in hindsight, were actually just us fumbling around, assuming with our limited knowledge that it constituted sex, then proudly peeling off our virgin labels. I would suspect Aidan thinks of me as his first love but not the one to take his virginity. This left me unknowingly naive and ill-equipped when I found myself in Reed's bed for the first time. It was as though I'd been dropped into the deep end where I plunged low. Surrounded by the smell of burning incense, I lay still, too nervous to make any wrong moves and too embarrassed to admit I didn't know what to do. What could be less attractive? Or so I thought.

Reed looked older than twenty-four, worlds away from my introductory experiences with Aidan. His extra years had transformed him from a bony teenager to a broad young man in his twenties. Before me was a different specimen, and I was without training wheels. Unaware of the impact of this moment, I worried only about looking cool. His stubble scraped my face like sandpaper; he had wide, tattooed shoulders and actual chest hair. I was a guppy — curve-free, lingering teenage acne and baby fat in all the wrong places. Reed's body didn't feel like one of a fellow teenager. Part of me was painfully embarrassed, unsure if he'd ever invite me over again. But I wanted him since I first laid eyes on him and now, I'd spent the night in his dark lair. In his bed. I floated through the rest of the day.

Your words don't haunt me. You forcing sex on me doesn't haunt me. You making me hate myself — that haunts me. You wanted to break me down so I didn't have the confidence to leave you.

CHAPTER 2

Over the next few weeks, we saw Reed at the bar every once in a while, usually with his friend Ben. Ben was tall and thin with pale skin and a face like John Lennon. His hair was dark and shoulder-length. I'd learn that Ben and Reed were similar creatures, both beautifully jaded. Each with their own demons and complications, Ben was gentler, a romantic who couldn't help but fall in love, inevitably ending up with a broken heart. Reed, on the other hand, would never fall in love.

Thankfully I was always equipped with my secret weapon — Marley. Her fearlessness and disinterest in Reed or Ben romantically made it easy for her. She welcomed herself into their booth, flashing me a quick, proud smirk.

But it never led anywhere.

I wondered out loud to Marley, "I guess that side of us is over, we're just neighbours now. Maybe he's dating someone else."

"I don't know, but I doubt it," Marley said.

"Really?"

"Yeah, I bet we would have seen that."

"I just think he's the most good-looking person I've ever seen." My mind wandered.

"I know you do. That's funny. I don't see him that way at all," Marley said.

Then one night just as I was just drifting off to sleep, my phone vibrated. I turned over to see Reed's name.

Sleepover?

I unlocked my front door.

Not ten minutes later, with his black hood up, he was sliding into bed next to me. Without a word, he buried his face into my neck and placed a familiar arm across my body. Just like that, I was back in it.

Reed began coming over every once in a while, instances growing more frequent over time. Late at night, my phone would vibrate and I buzzed him into the building. His low voice whispered, "Hi." He'd lie with his arms around me, maybe fall asleep for a while. Then he'd leave again, back to whatever he did throughout his insomniac nights: smoking, reading, listening to music. Things looked a bit different when it was me doing the sneaking down the block. Standing frozen in my bedroom, I'd wait for a burst of courage to text. Although he often did the same, Reed's life was somehow much more off-limits. I was never sure if he actually wanted me there or if he perpetually preferred to be alone. Somehow, even after weeks of sharing a bed, I still felt like a desperate intruder. The only time my heavy uncertainty eased was while we were having sex. Sex meant I was contributing something, earning my place in his bed, in his world. Though, when we were in the dark and tucked under layers of sheets, Reed saw me as a dimensional person with interests and opinions, not simply convenient as I feared. One night, as the heat of anxiety was inching its way up my neck, Reed assured me he'd never let anything happen to me. As the rest of the city slept, for the tiniest moment in time, I could have sworn he was mine. I forced my stinging eyes to stay awake. Lying next to Reed, sleep was wasted time.

Undetected and after hours, our addiction to each other grew. In the exposing daylight, we hid it all. We didn't touch each other, we didn't tell anyone. He went out; I went out. We rarely spent time alone until the sun went down. Once it was dark and if either of us was lonely, we made our way down the street and into each other's beds. We talked about the Beatles, watched more music documentaries, and laughed. I crawled into the nook under his arm and tried to stop my heart from beating too obviously against his bare chest.

"So, what do you think is *actually* going on between you two? Are you like . . . together?" Marley asked once we'd been sneaking into each other's rooms for some time. I was sitting in front of a full-length mirror as she stood above me braiding my bangs.

"We're definitely not together. I don't think it's anything real."

Marley narrowed her eyes. "But do you think he sees it that way?" she asked.

"For sure. Reed will never be anyone's boyfriend, that guy is like a ghost. I've barely seen him in the daylight."

"That is true, but I don't know, Cal. You might mean more to him than you think," Marley warned.

"I don't think so. We don't even speak unless we're alone."

"But that's just because you're both weird and don't know how to handle it. He doesn't spend time with anyone he doesn't want to spend time with. He chooses to come over and see you. He wants to hang out with you. I don't know why you don't see it." She spoke through the bobby pin pinched between her lips.

"So, what am I supposed to do? I can't be like, 'What are we?' If he says something I don't want to hear . . . That's a nightmare."

"Ask him!" She looked at me through the mirror with wide eyes.

"Absolutely not."

Marley and I spent every minute together in that little downtown apartment. And pretty quickly, any boundaries between her and me ceased to exist. We shared all our clothes, often slept in the same bed, and no conversations were off-limits. We had a little family in the city made up of each other and a small group of friends from school. Typical Friday nights looked like this: once our lectures and six-hour painting studios were finished, we would cross the street to a Chinese restaurant that served impossibly cheap beer. From there, we all made our way to the corner bar. Risking her annoyance, I would often make Marley text Reed to join us. And to my surprise, occasionally, he, and Ben, would. At the bar, Reed and I had our little ways of acknowledging we weren't just friends, while still walking our fine line. He put his hand on my knee under the table, and I put my hand on his. He texted me a heart. We had our own exciting world bubbling just beneath the surface of an already exciting one.

On one of those Friday nights, from the other side of a table full of nachos, Marley opened the camera on her phone and gestured to Reed and I, "Smile, you two!"

I tensed, unsure just how cozy we should get.

"Put your hand down my shirt," Reed said.

"What?" We never touched each other in public. And it was a strange ask.

Reed pulled the collar of his brown ripped T-shirt low and nodded in my direction. I stuck my hand down the neck and onto his chest. Reed tilted his head back and closed his eyes, I smiled, Marley took the photo.

"Weirdos. Okay, now do something else. Just smile, you guys! It's okay to like each other!" Marley could say anything and it was never weird. Reed leaned his head against my shoulder and smiled with his eyes closed. I felt my face flush warm and hid under my scarf. She snapped another photo.

Eventually, it reached last call and after laughing for hours in a graffitied booth filled with guacamole remnants and empty beer glasses, the four of us headed home. Some nights, Reed would disappear to his apartment alone. Other nights, he and I would head up the fire escape together. Then there were the nights we each withdrew into our own bedrooms, and a couple hours later, my phone vibrated.

I was sleeping next to someone complicated. I had no idea how to do "casual," or really, how to interact with him at all. Every conversation left me feeling like I was about fourteen talking to the most popular twelfth grader. I needed Marley around to inject energy, putting my nerves at ease. She'd burst into the kitchen wearing a lace dress and a huge smile, "Hello! What's going on? How are my broodiest friends?" Reed would smile back at her, as if admiring her ability to be loud, outwardly warm, and joyful. I felt the need to be subtle and low-key to match his overall simmer. Reed spent most days working at a nearby camera store, and nights editing photographs or sketching, listening to Syd Barrett or Circa Survive. He scribbled in a small dream journal. He read a lot, often books about spirituality, then smoked weed and watched movies I'd never heard of. He wasn't the guy you'd invite to a Halloween party or take a selfie with. He responded to simple questions like, "So do you want photography to be your whole career?," with something non-committal and crushingly cool like, "Tomorrow never knows."

I knew Reed was home when his door was propped open an inch. Every afternoon on my way to class, my eyes would dart to his door, clocking whether or not he was home, as if my life depended on it. Some weeks I barely saw him until he appeared in my bed in the middle of the night. Other days I'd be sitting at his kitchen table while he made us spaghetti, *Sgt. Pepper* blasting from his room, filling the apartment. He was a tough person to get to know, and although I was beginning to understand his different laughs and memorize his favourite records, I didn't know much about him at all.

I understand how people become addicts. Anything to stop me from thinking. Anything to stop the memories. They're haunting me. I want to empty my mind. I want to erase my memory.

CHAPTER 3

My life changed when I was seventeen. One moment I was sitting on my bed chatting with Aidan on the phone, and the next, I was pacing in the snow wearing just pyjama shorts and a tank top, feeling like I was about to faint or throw up or maybe both.

"What are you feeling? Are you sick? What do you think it is?" My mom asked. My parents trailed behind me as I looped through the house.

"I don't know, I don't know. Something is wrong."

"Do we need to bring you to the hospital?" My mom wasn't an alarmist.

"I don't know. I don't think so. I can't tell if I'm sick or if I'm going to faint. I can't tell." Pins and needles tickled my fingertips.

"Come here. Try sitting down. Let me feel your forehead."

I tried to sit, but my legs sprang back up.

"I can't. I feel like I can't breathe. I can't sit down." I continued to pace the living room.

"You're okay, Honey," my dad's steady voice cut through my fear. "You're going to be fine."

It was a few hours before I was calm enough to lie down. I climbed into my parents' bed and waited for my body to feel like my own. Waves of fear crashed into me, launching me forward. My mom quietly brought me back down.

"Relax your toes. Relax your feet. Relax your knees. Your legs. Your hips. Your stomach. Relax your shoulders." My mom whispered to me once all the lights were out. We worked our way up my body, and together, we both relaxed. That night, I slept cocooned between my parents.

Days later, once we realized it was a panic attack, my mom began reading about anxiety and panic. We sat together at the kitchen island one afternoon when I should have been in school. With a gentle voice, she told me that according to her research, "It may never happen again, or it may become an ongoing thing in your life." Not long after, I started having panic attacks every day.

Anxiety flipped my life upside down. It was the late 2000s, and these things weren't talked about. I sat in my parents' bed watching the same two movies, drinking lemon water, and eating nothing but raw vegetables and mint Fisherman's Friends — inexplicably the only things that didn't scare me. If I did manage to muster up the courage to leave the safety of home, I pictured myself vomiting, paced in tight circles, and hit myself on the chest over and over to release some of the toxic energy pulsing through my body. Most of the time, my parents would pick me up, and soon I'd be back in their bed, licking my wounds to the same two movies.

Aidan was kind and patient. He tried to understand, which was impressive for a teenage boy. He rescued me from the movie theatre when I was panicking mid-show, he talked to me on the phone from across the world when I was panicking in the middle of the night, and he never seemed to mind that we didn't go to many parties — or really do much of anything — because my anxiety was too debilitating.

It was a Friday night in, fighting flickering waves of familiar panic. It's where so much of my energy went. I sat on my bed watching the latest episode of *Dexter*, ignoring the mountain of assignments I should have been working on. Marley was at her boyfriend's, the rest of my friends seemingly busy. I hoped to spend time with Reed on the weekend, especially nights like these when I was home alone with anxiety. So, I did something I didn't often do; I texted him and initiated real plans together.

Do you want to go to the corner tonight?

After a couple of long minutes, he wrote back, *I do, I'm with Ben. How's 9?*

I checked the time. 7:09 p.m.

Sounds good.

I stayed curled in bed for another hour.

Stomach heavy with dread and sadness, I eventually peeled myself out from under the covers and examined my face in the mirror. Familiar dark purple bags lined my under eyes.

After fighting with a pair of sheer black tights, I grabbed a tight black skirt and threw on oversized sweater. I smeared some Maybelline foundation across my face, adding an extra layer under my eyes.

It was December. The city was cold but alive. I opened the door to the busiest I'd ever seen our corner bar. Packed, noisy and overwhelming.

Slipping through the crowd, I scanned each booth for Reed's messy black hair. Until finally, I spotted him.

In the back booth, where I'd met him for the very first time, Reed sat smiling with his eyes down. Next to him was a girl with long, dark hair. I froze. And watched. Reed looked over at her, put a hand around the back of her neck and kissed her.

The roaring laughter and chaotic chatter around me went quiet, and my feet felt super-glued to the sticky floor. My brain pleaded with me to move, to lift each foot and go home.

We weren't a couple — nowhere near it — I wasn't allowed to be angry.

But he was expecting me.

From the day we met, something about him made me feel small. A fearful voice inside my head said he wanted me purely out of convenience, that he'd always have other options, maybe more than most considering his Prince of Grunge good looks and brutal aloofness. But I also believed, at the very least, he saw something special in the friendship he had with both Marley and me. I believed he didn't want to hurt either of us.

Marley came home from her boyfriend's the next afternoon. Before she could even take her shoes off, I rushed her into my room and sat her down on my bed.

"I've been texting you. I have to tell you what happened last night," my voice was almost panicked.

"My phone is dead. What happened?" She unhooked her purse from her shoulder and stared back at me.

"Reed told me to meet him at the corner and when I got there, he was kissing some girl." My throat seized.

"Are you kidding me? Who is she? Did you meet her?"

"I have no idea. I didn't speak to either of them."

"So you haven't heard from him today either?"

"No, nothing."

A few days passed, and we hadn't crossed paths. I hadn't heard from him. I wasn't sure if he was avoiding me or if his legs were somewhere wrapped in hers. One morning, after a two-hour art history lecture, I came home to an empty apartment. Without the constant activity of Marley, the apartment felt eerie. Almost unknown. I took off all my clothes and had a long, searing hot shower. I was still in a fog after what I'd seen. And I knew, being neighbours, I'd have to face him eventually. The shower was a little vacation from the reality that was leaving me trapped and repeatedly reminded.

But soon, my fingers were wrinkled and my feet were swollen and red, so I pulled myself out from under the hot water and wrapped myself in a big towel. I stood staring into the misty mirror, when a gentle knock quietly rattled my front door.

I opened the door to Reed's green eyes.

"Hey. You scared me!"

I didn't mean to say those words, or any words. We hadn't spoken in days. He looked back at me. The apartment was quiet, nothing but the distant hum of traffic on the other side of the thick glass windows. Reed threw his arms around me — soaking wet and in a towel — and hugged me tight, leading me backwards into the apartment. I felt his heart beating. With his arms around me and his face buried in my neck, he whispered, "I'm so sorry."

After a few seconds, I hesitantly hugged him back, but was careful not to give quite as much.

"Can we talk?" His eyes focused intensely.

I paused, then reluctantly said, "Sure. Let me put some clothes on." Reed followed me into my bedroom.

My heart thumped. I threw on leggings and a leopard print sweater. With my hair still dripping, I sat down beside him, but farther away than I would have the week before. Sitting next to Reed was uncomfortable, even awkward now. Not long before, he was the only thing that eased the relentlessness of my sadness. Now he was a stranger.

"I'm sorry for what happened. It wasn't nice. I wasn't thinking." He chose his words carefully, keeping them as vague as we were.

"Well . . . I'm not sure what to say. You're allowed to do it. I don't really have the right to be mad. You can do whatever you want, we *both* —" I couldn't resist peppering in a small threat.

"No, I get why you're mad."

"I know it's complicated, but that was a blatant disregard for my feelings." I still hadn't looked at him. Reed and I shared a long pause before his voice appeared once again.

"The good news is, Callie, I hate myself more than you could ever hate me."

Though not emphatically, Reed was apologizing the only way he knew how, by underlining his self-contempt. It was the closest we had come to admitting any real feelings existed between us, the first time I was ever angry with him. The first time I hinted at how deeply I cared for him, and him for me. We sat one foot apart, talking in circles for so long the sun had gone down and Marley was buzzing around the kitchen. Lulls in our weary conversation were now filled with the rattling of kitchen drawers and cutlery. Eventually, we both ran out of things to say or new ways to say them. Reed lay down. He asked me to lie down with him. I said no.

He tried again. "Please. Lie down with me."

"No. I don't want to."

I continued to stare forward, not yet ready to look at him. His eyes would make me give in. Then he wrapped his hands around my shoulders and pulled me down toward the bed. Something inside of me winced. It felt a little bit too hard.

Small moments like these are impossibly difficult to label, especially without the context of what happens next. Yes, he pulled me down toward the bed a bit too hard, but he didn't threaten me. I wasn't scared. It was just small enough that I was left with only the quietest doubt, and just strange enough to always remember.

Every night, I swallow a little pill so that I'll want to stay alive. But it doesn't always work.

CHAPTER 4

In my late twenties, I was on my way to my parents' house when I got a text from my dad that said, *We were robbed.* I opened the text to photos of wreckage: destroyed kitchen cabinets, clothes ripped from hangers, pieces of my dad's collectibles on the ground in the garage. I drove up the gravel driveway not long after, already in tears. This was my fear since my parents decided to move to such a secluded area. Whenever I was alone in the house at night, I hid on the ground in the kitchen, back planted firmly against the cabinets where no one could see me through the black windows. My family did their best to assure me we were safer there than we were in the city, but my imagination ran rampant each night we were without streetlights or neighbours.

That day, we walked through the house in silence examining seemingly endless damage. Photos of our family thrown from the walls, every drawer emptied. The bedrooms where my sisters and I had spent our teenage years were turned upside down. All my mother's jewellery was stolen. I was scared to be alone, worried whoever did this was still there, hiding. I hated feeling violated inside the walls of our own home, angry someone could ruin this thing that never belonged to them. It wasn't theirs to take.

Before the break-in, that house was where I felt most calm, my favourite escape from the demons I'd always wrestled. It was Christmases, birthdays, sad days, happy days, movie nights, sick days, friends, family, boyfriends. But after that day, it would forever feel a little bit less ours. It's a very specific sadness — that feeling when someone you knew so well, or a place that felt so safe only days ago, suddenly feels wrong.

Reed was trying to right that feeling, to change my mind back and make me feel close to him again. He knew just what would work. Arms full of groceries, I came home to a piece of paper taped to my front door. Knowing exactly who it was from, I tingled with excitement. The little folded paper contained a drawing of a man sitting at a table, cutting into a big piece of steak. In the other corner, a flying cat. The words, *Dinner? My treat*, were written across the top in the microscopic boyish scribble every girl knows.

Reed and I had never been on a "date." Our relationship started with a *do you wanna watch a movie* text and carried on because our drunken nights out inevitably ended with us at the same bar where it was all too easy to stumble into each other's beds. But a dinner date? That was odd and even, potentially, awkward. I snipped the labels off a terracotta Aritzia dress, curled my hair, and slid into black tights. The sky would burst with snow any day now. I was giddy. Leaving the apartment for a date felt so new, it was as if we'd just met with a glistening clean slate.

We hopped the streetcar to one of my favourite Italian restaurants in the east end where he made us a reservation. Shoulder to shoulder on the streetcar's velvet seats, I looked over at his black hair, barely contained under a black toque, and said, "It's starting to feel like Christmas."

We barely spent any time vertical just the two of us. I wasn't used to touching him, talking to him, or looking at him alone and out in the world. As we watched downtown fly by and I worked hard to contain my smile, Reed muttered under his breath, "Kill me now."

Later that weekend, I had the apartment to myself. With no one to hide from, I was excited to see what would happen. Would he come over, would we exist like a real couple — eat dinner at the table, turn the lights out together and wake up together, brush our teeth both still in our underwear? There was no reason for us to sneak around. We didn't have to wait for our bedroom doors to shut before letting smiles slip out.

My mind pulsed with pain as I lay staring at the ceiling, eyes heavy with dread. It's a feeling that had become routine. My brain swirled, searching for any small relief from the sadness and worrying. *I should have run for longer at the gym today, my anxiety will never get better, he doesn't love me, he'll never love me, I'll never feel happy, bad things will happen to me.* I reached for Tylenol Cold Nighttime to knock myself out. I had no interest in anything stronger; I just needed to fall asleep, stay asleep, and forget how bad I felt when I was awake. I gulped down the big, blue pills and waited.

My phone rang.

"Hi," I answered and sat up halfway, worried he could somehow sense my depression looming low in the air.

"Hi." Not five minutes later, Reed climbed into bed beside me. Leaving my bedroom door open, he draped an arm around me and I stared at his hand, the sleeves of his black hoodie a bit too long for his arms. I played with his thin yarn bracelets and regretted the Tylenol.

"Are you going to sleep now?" His voice told me his eyes were closed.

"Maybe. Why?"

"I thought we could watch *Blow*, that Johnny Depp movie I was talking about."

I smiled into the darkness and we both lay still, listening to each other's breaths. His hand scooped around my body, gently holding my rib cage.

"I don't want to be with anyone else," Reed said quietly. I squeezed his arm. "Do you understand?"

"Understand what?"

"How much you mean to me," he said.

I told him, "I don't know, you tell me."

"I don't want to be with anyone else." He paused for a moment before emphasizing, "Ever."

It was after nights like these that my hopes would rise, telling me maybe, just maybe, Reed really did love me. Maybe he'd become a constant, safe place to undo my sadness. But he wasn't built that way. He treasured his independence, guarding it with such ferocity it was as if he'd cease to exist without it. I was reminded of this with an empty seat at the breakfast table.

I can't stand to look at myself in the mirror. I hate showering—I don't want to see my body.

CHAPTER 5

February reading week was just days away. It felt as if the sun never reached our apartment at all, the city too cold to walk even the shortest blocks. In a few days, I'd be miles away in the Virgin Islands.

When I went home to my parents' for a weekend here and there over the last few months, I didn't hear from Reed much, if at all. The absolute most was a text with just a heart, which I took as his way of telling me he was still there. I never reached out to him, either. The fear of his particular rejection froze my fingers, perhaps protecting me from the disappointment I believed would inevitably come.

Leading up to the break, I'd been trying to figure out what to do with my puppy, Dexter, while I was away. We lay in bed one frigid evening and Reed said, "I'll take him."

"Really?" My eyes lit up.

"Yeah. It'll be nice to have him," he said. "Dex is an old soul. I bet he'd like my dad's dog. Maybe they can meet."

A few days later, I gave Dex a hug, thanked Reed again, and met my family at the airport.

Over the next week, my depression ached, relentless and inescapable. I lay awake watching palm tree shadows sway, writing in a black Moleskine journal and berating myself with insults. *I'm gaining too much weight. I don't deserve breakfast. I want to die.* I wished to claw myself out of the dark spiral or out of my own skin. My eyes darted across every inch of my body, lingering on each piece I thought should be slimmer, daintier, more attractive. I did my best to shower without looking at my naked self, willing my thighs to be thinner, my hair to be longer, my skin to be clearer. Why couldn't I have fewer beauty marks and hair on my arms? I hated the roll that appeared on my stomach when I sat down.

My family ate at candlelit, white tablecloth restaurants overlooking the ocean. I eyed their fresh rolls, clam chowder, steak frites, and crème brûlée. In front of me, just a starter salad. Enough of us were there, I could hide. Maybe if I came back from vacation skinny, I would finally find some peace, pushing away the dark cloud. Maybe he'd want me a little bit more. Maybe I'd even have the energy to find someone else.

On top of hating my body and depriving myself of food, I fought off thoughts of self-harming all day and throughout every long night I spent awake. It was the closest I'd come to wanting to take my own life. Immense guilt came with these immense thoughts. I wrote myself reminders: *I'm the luckiest girl in the world. I'm away with my parents, sisters, and grandparents in a beautiful house on a cliff overlooking the ocean. It's a trip many only do once in their lives, if ever. I have parents who would want to know that I'm struggling. If I tell them, they'll help.* I had everything I could have ever wanted or needed to succeed. And yet, my heart was heavy and my ankles were weighted. My body hurt as I dragged it through the motions of living, of pretending to be happy, while secretly staring over the edge of a building. How could I tell anyone I wanted to die when my life was so easy? So privileged. Justifying my sadness was impossible.

Occasionally, I got a message from Reed. He sent me pictures of Dex running in his parents' backyard. Reed was the light at the end of the tunnel. Soon, I would be back in his orbit, numbing my pain, addicted to his inconsistencies. Maybe *then* I'd feel better.

I touched down in Toronto at ten p.m. As I crept through the city in heavy Saturday night traffic, I texted Reed: *Just landed. Are you home? I'll pop by for Dex.*

Reed replied quickly: *Yep, we're here.*

After throwing my suitcase into my own apartment, I flung myself back down the stairs and ran around the corner. Glancing up at the fire escape, Reed's lights were on, his door no longer propped open in the February snow.

I knocked lightly and waited. When no one answered, I opened the door slowly looking around the small living room. Dex was sleeping on Reed's creaky blue futon. I ran over and hugged him tight. He was nothing more than a little ball of fur staring at me with round, wet eyes.

"I'm so sorry for leaving you."

With Dex still in my arms, I made my way across the apartment to Reed's bedroom. The anticipation of seeing him again had built inside of me over the last forty-eight hours. Maybe he would be relieved to see me, too. But when I got to his door, I found him sitting on the edge of the bed next to a girl. A different girl.

"Hi." It was all that came out of my mouth. My jaw began to tremble.

"Oh, hey. I didn't hear you come in. How was the trip?" His words were light and floating, free of guilt.

"It was good . . . I'm Callie." My arms went weak. I gripped Dex.

"Yeah, sorry, this is Adrienne," he said. "She's, uh, my friend from home."

Adrienne smiled. "Hi."

"When did you guys get here?" I tried to fill in some blanks.

"We drove down this morning. I have my dad's car." His eyes were cluelessly cruel.

"Dex is so cute," Adrienne said. She had a beautiful French accent. Reed was wearing one of his striped T-shirts I sometimes slept in. I shrank into my shoulders.

"Okay, well. Thanks again for watching Dex. I hope he was good."

"Ya, no problem." Reed looked up at me. "Welcome home."

I was intruding. It was obvious what would happen once I left and they turned out the lights. I couldn't ask to speak with him in the hall, and I couldn't stare at him with hurt eyes. I knew what was expected of me and it was nothing; do nothing, say nothing. That's the role of the unbothered girl. The one who casually sleeps with the older guy, the one who shrugs at no rules, the one deemed "cool." They don't get their feelings hurt.

This particular feeling, the one where you're made to feel crazy, is one most women experience at some point in their dating lives. You know, the one where you're told one thing and shown the opposite. At eighteen, the ridiculousness was lost on me. So was the manipulation.

Back in my own apartment, I peeled off my armour. Immediately, panicked thoughts began to pick up speed, and I felt the train coming off the tracks. Fearing what I might do to myself and sick at the thought of having to sleep alone, I called my parents.

"Hi, Honey." My dad answered on speaker phone.

"Hi, Dad. Um—" My voice cracked.

Immediately concerned, my dad asked, "What's wrong, Honey?"

"Can you come get me? I just can't be here. I have to get out of my apartment. Can you guys come and get me, please?" The hot tears were coming.

My mom's comforting voice appeared. "We're still on our way home from the airport. What's going on?"

"I just need to come home."

"Okay, well, we can come get you first thing in the morning, how's that?" She said. Maybe I'd feel better once I got *there*, but until then, I couldn't be alone in my apartment. My friend came over to pick me up. We threw some clothes in a backpack, grabbed Dex, and left for her condo. Dex and I slept on her couch that night. I checked my phone obsessively, hoping his name would appear, lighting up the dark living room. Shame radiated through me as I remembered all that had kept me alive the last few weeks was knowing Reed had my dog and believing we were making progress. How pathetic. I knew I couldn't stay alive just for a bad boy. I needed something else to numb it all.

Tempting as it was to blame him, Reed wasn't the cause of my depression. But my days being intimately interwoven with his, plus the heavy burden of just existing, and our vague relationship, it all became one giant cloud of indecipherable sadness. On days I felt particularly low, I unfairly — and immaturely — looked to Reed for comfort when he wasn't equipped to help me. I expected him to just *know* he was something that made me feel good at a time when nothing else did. But he didn't know, and I never told him.

It's hard to recognize myself in this person who relied so heavily on a boy for their happiness. But at eighteen, while my self-assurance was in its infancy, I looked externally.

I began acting out in ways that were entirely out of character. In the middle of the night, if I couldn't cope with the loudness of my brain any longer, I walked to my parents' empty condo, leaving my phone at home and disappearing into the city. I didn't care if something happened to me while I walked empty streets, alone, in the dark. In fact, I almost welcomed it. Being physically hurt would have helped me when I didn't have the language.

Every choice reflected how badly I wanted to escape my own life and pathetic body. I avoided sleeping in my own bed, I didn't wear my own clothes, and being around my family and friends only plunged me lower. I hated being inside of my skin, so I tried to alter it with tattoos, by changing the colour of my hair or, in my worst moments, cutting my inner arms and ankles, my newly discovered favourite punishment. I ran from any reminder I was the permanent protagonist of my life, inescapably chained down by unrelenting sadness. Reed and our painful, blurry relationship weren't the causes of my depression; I was depressed long before that first night that we spent by the glow of flickering candles. But the thick toxicity between us didn't help as I became too tired to keep treading water. When I couldn't find happiness in anything else, my self-esteem and mood began to hinge entirely on Reed and his exclusive attention. It was beginning to cost me every sliver of joy I had left.

Twice burned, I lived in constant fear of seeing Reed with someone else. So, when our school term sublet was up, it was a perfect time for Marley and me to leave this apartment behind and start fresh in a new neighbourhood.

"This will be good for us," Marley said, as she folded her collection of floral dresses.

"I feel like Reed is mad at me right now," I told her. "The air is weird and we aren't speaking anymore."

"Well, you didn't do anything wrong. Reed is the one who should feel bad."

"But, like, he didn't technically do anything wrong and that's why it's confusing. He was allowed to do those things . . . It isn't his fault I'm hurt. I don't know. I kinda had a thing with that guy Evan from class, remember? Maybe that was just as bad."

"Cal, those aren't comparable. Nothing even happened with that guy. Reed is messing with you. He isn't being careful about it, either. He isn't treating you well, and I don't think you're in a place to handle it right now. I mean, you shouldn't have to handle it ever, but especially now. You know? Don't blame yourself."

Eventually, news of our imminent move made its way to Reed. I waited to cross paths over a tense drink in our crowded corner bar.

I thought about how I'd explain it, if I'd admit that it was mostly born out of my desire to stop seeing him. But instead, Reed disappeared, and I left without saying goodbye.

During our last few days in the apartment, partway through packing our bedrooms into Rubbermaid boxes, we came home to a hole kicked into our front door. There was only one person we suspected.

"This is a huge overreaction." Marley's voice remained steady.

It was a threat, a scary threat, as Reed tested boundaries by dipping his toe into violence. My willingness to brush his behaviour aside is strange, and I find my own actions confusing. I'd never experienced any sort of violence before the hole in my door, and, to my mature mind, I can't understand how it didn't scare me to death. I chalk it up to blissful naïveté, still unaware of the true threat of men, without my antennas precisely attuned to whispers of danger. I'd never had to be aware, leaving these particular senses underdeveloped.

As we moved into our new apartment, I also decided to drop out of school. My mental health wasn't allowing me to keep up with classes, and it all started to slip away. Eventually, I couldn't get it back. One day just before the move, I was walking to class. When I reached the turn for school, my feet just kept walking as if on their own rescue mission. Before I knew it, I was at my dad's office. When I got to his door, he was on the phone. I knocked quietly and he waved me in. I sat myself down on the couch, admiring the coziness of this place I knew so well and waited for his call to end. Finally, he hung up the phone and said, "Hi, Honey! What's going on?" It all spilled out.

"I'm not enjoying school, Dad. It isn't going well. I'm not getting good grades, I'm not happy, I'm not even good at what I'm doing. I don't think it's the right place for me."

Without hesitation, he said, "Okay. Do you want to give it a little bit longer, or do you feel like you've made a decision?" His calmness helped my lungs to relax.

"I don't want to do it anymore. It doesn't feel right."

"Okay, well, don't worry. These things happen. We'll figure out what's next. Should we call your mom?"

"Sure." I sat amongst the comfort of my dad's successful career and wondered if I would have one of my own. Only a few days later, I was in line at the Administrations Office.

There was probably much more to it, but I remember the conversation like this.

"I want to drop out. How do I . . . How do I actually drop out?" I asked a bored-looking woman behind the desk. She handed me a form used for dropping classes.

"Fill this out but write in all of your classes."

"So, if I drop all my classes, I'll have 'dropped out'?"

"Yep."

She also let me know that within a certain amount of time I could re-register and finish my degree if I changed my mind. If that window expired, I would have to reapply.

When I got home, I proudly taped the dropout paperwork to my bedroom wall. I was moving on from the things that weren't right.

SURVIVING

Why did he bring me back in, just to to do this to me all over again.
Why couldn't he have just let me go.

CHAPTER 6

Toronto was alive in a way only warm weather brings. The waterfront was full of joggers, sidewalks were buzzing with patio drinkers and pitchers of beer. Two months had passed since Marley and I moved. I'd had a birthday, cut my hair to my chin, and taken up a new hobby of collecting records. But I couldn't escape his face; every dark-haired guy with over-ear headphones and tattooed arms was him. My heart stopped each time I heard the rattling wheels of a skateboard skipping over city curbs. Yet, even while I hoped for his familiar face and plaid shirts in every crowd, part of me believed I'd never see him again and knew it was for the better. My parents were growing increasingly concerned about me. You can only call home asking to be picked up, then sit in the basement without eating, so many times before they catch on that something is seriously wrong. My parents also received two separate phone calls from my closest friends who were independently concerned I might harm myself. Identifying the monster was important to my parents. They needed to name it, a targeted enemy that we could band together and defeat, before deciding how to help. The only one I could name was Reed and my hurt feelings, so I let my parents believe he was the sole problem, and now, I would start to feel better.

Marley sprinkled her magic and our apartment became a home. A happy home. A safe place. She bought flowers, hung paintings, and lit candles. It was a time of change. Our new apartment was starting to feel like one of two nineteen-year-old girls, bursting with colour, music, and life. We had friends over for pre-drinks and birthdays. Marley threw dinner parties, making us delicious meals followed by homemade cupcakes smothered in icing she made from scratch.

During one of those dinner parties, after a few glasses of wine, my friend Carter and I stood leaning against the kitchen counter.

"So, Marley kind of mentioned. Are you and that guy Reed done? What's happening there? Last time I was at your apartment you said you guys were still kind of seeing each other." He asked, eyeing me before taking a sip.

"Yeah, we're not seeing each other anymore. It got bad, which is kind of why we moved."

This was dicey territory a few drinks in. Just the mention of his name and my throat seized. No one could compare to him, but I couldn't explain why. Without Reed around, it didn't matter how I looked, who came over, if the guy from class texted me.

"That's too bad," Carter said, "He's gorgeous."

"Yeah . . ." I paused and looked at Carter. He was experienced, older, and he knew stuff. Plus, I was just the right level of buzzed. So, I asked, "You know, something weird happened. We had a bit of a fight one night, and after we were done talking, he put his hands on my shoulders and pulled me down toward the bed. I felt like he pulled me down kind of hard. Do you think that's . . . I don't know . . . Weird?"

"Nah, people do much worse."

I took another sip of wine. "Yeah. Anyway, that's enough about him. To sum up, no, we aren't seeing each other or whatever." I faked a shrug.

I started going to the gym every morning and jogging to the water every evening, each day calculating whether my thighs felt farther apart. If anyone asked, I would have said it was all to make myself feel healthier, to get things back on track. But in reality, I was punishing myself and my body, the body I deemed not good enough. Not perfect enough. Not fit enough, tanned enough, skinny enough. If I wasn't close to passing out or throwing up at the end of my run, I wasn't running hard enough.

Then one day in early June, Reed's name appeared in my email.

> *You are perfect, yes, it's true.*
> *But without me, you're only you.*
> *Do you still have room underneath your skin?*
> *I'm done torturing myself on everyone's behalf.*
> *Let me in?*

Attachment: A black and white photo he'd taken of me.

It was the last thing I expected. Never did I think I would hear from him, especially asking to be let back into my life. Reed liked me off-balance and inferior. Asking to see me didn't fit his pattern. It was exactly what I needed to see.

A few days later, I wrote: *I miss you.*

He replied: *Let's be bad.*

Nervous excitement rolled through me as I got dressed, a perfect cocktail of dread and butterflies. I wore the outfit I felt prettiest in, a black dress and black strappy sandals. I didn't share my plans with anyone. No one was there to join in my giddiness or assure me it wasn't a horrible mistake. Marley was working at a camp for the summer, so I could see him without anyone knowing. If it was a mistake, no one would ever have to know. It was the first thing I'd ever done entirely by myself, for myself.

We decided to meet outside our old corner bar, and as I made my way there, it was as though I'd successfully turned back time. And yet, everything had changed. This time it was clear: We were meeting because we missed each other. We were acknowledging feelings. We wanted to be together, and it overpowered my logical brain.

Our city was busy and heavy with heat. I weaved through families and students on the sidewalk, past small store displays of sunglasses and juicy fruit. My feet moved, quick and light, dodging fellow city walkers while trying to stay relaxed.

I turned the final corner and there he was, waiting across the street. Tall, dark Reed. We hugged on the sidewalk. I wasn't sure we'd ever hugged before. Touching him while standing was strange, like a brand-new body I didn't know. My hands lingered on his shoulders just for a moment.

"Wow. It's so weird to see you," I told him.

He flashed a dark smile and I checked on the tiny gap between his front teeth. "So. What do you wanna do?"

"I don't know . . . What do *you* wanna do?" Suggesting one of our apartments seemed heavy, sudden. But sitting amongst people, at the bar, at the park, was wrong.

"Let's go to my place," he said.

I was gambling with the loss of Marley who may not want to watch a repeat from the sidelines. And my family, who believed I should know better and stay away from this person who, given many opportunities, had never chosen me. But his addition was enough to make up for the loss. I studied him: the backs of his tattooed arms, the veins in his hands, the way he barely picked up his knees as he walked. I could finally breathe again. Shoulder to shoulder, we walked. I'd never met warm-weather Reed; his signature black hair was trimmed much shorter, and he was wearing black denim shorts, a thin black T-shirt, and dark sunglasses. I followed him up a fire escape, and just like that, I was back in the ring.

The city heat had risen to Reed's small, top-floor apartment. I sat myself down on the creaky blue futon and looked around the living room. Records, amps, books, and empty beer bottles all lay scattered about. I wasn't sure what to do with my arms, with my purse, or how comfortable I should get. He would always be that boy from the bar.

Reed was standing in front of me, broad shoulders leaning against the frame his bedroom door. The living room was safe. Neutral. If we stayed in the living room, I wasn't doing anything wrong. Not really.

"Never thought I'd be back here," I said, smile sneaking through.

"I wasn't sure either," Reed looked back at me, chewing the inside of his cheek. He disappeared into his bedroom and returned with the the photograph he'd emailed me. It was a photo he'd taken in his bedroom one sunny morning. I remembered the morning, wearing one of his *KISS* T-shirts, drinking coffee.

"I developed one of our pixie-dust girl, too," he said, and showed me an equally beautiful photograph of Marley. Immediately, the enormity of his gesture deflated. I gave up this whiplash cold turkey two months prior. Now, Reed was spoon-feeding me a little taste, inches from my face, with a look in his eye. I could never resist him. Not long after, I followed him into his bedroom.

Reed's bedroom looked brand-new. In the last two months, he'd taken down his photographs, painted it light blue and covered almost every inch with sketches of creatures and twisty song lyrics. A skateboard graveyard was tucked in the corner, a pair of black vintage Levi's folded on the bed. Reed's plaid comforter and beige sheets made me both warm and cold. I'd spent so much time in them already. My eyes darted up and down, side to side, scouring the walls. Everything was a piece of him.

In that bedroom, I would grow up and see how complicated the world can be.

"What have you been doing all summer?" He asked me as we sat on his bed.

"I'm looking for a summer job or else I'll have to go home. That's kinda the deal with my parents." I said, still examining the blue walls. "Are you still working at the store?"

"Yeah. Though I might say fuck it and move to Thailand or something. It's sucking the remnants of my already decrepit soul."

I smiled. A very Reed response.

The air around Reed was different — it was always different — fleeting and filled with both electricity and unease. I couldn't tell if he was never honest or always a bit too honest. Before Reed, I didn't know it was possible to feel so unsettled, yet comfortable at the same time. I knew what I was doing was wrong, and I knew I was playing with fire. My parents saw him as bad news, Marley thought I needed someone healthier, a sizeable part of me knew it was the wrong decision. I snuck back into his life completely under the radars of everyone who loved me. I'd never done anything like it, and it was awful. But so good. My obsession was stronger than ever, a thrill radiating through my body each time he looked at me. I could have crawled under his skin.

Eventually, we lay down on his bed. He said, "You got a new tattoo," and grazed my wrist. That was it. That's all it took for me to fall blissfully off the wagon. He seeped back into my veins, and I let the rest of my life drift away.

That summer was oppressively hot, and Reed's small top-floor apartment was even hotter. With no air conditioning and only one window in the blue bedroom, Reed and I spent that summer having sex, taking cold showers, and throwing on sandals to grab iced cappuccinos. The days were long in the best way. Endless sunlight meant hours to lie around trying to stay cool, yet still draping our limbs across each other's sticky bodies. The shorter hair made his dark eyebrows that much darker and his stunning features even more striking.

It was a slow, sunny morning as we made our way down the stairs of Reed's apartment. We passed an older man and immediately,

Reed's face lit up. He was never able to hide when he really liked someone. His big smile was suddenly unbridled, and yet still, his desire to conceal his own happiness was unmissable.

"This is my landlord — the guy I've been telling you about," Reed said to me, flashing his illusive toothy grin. He'd told me all about his landlord and what an interesting person he was. "This is my girlfriend, Callie. I just wanted you to know who it was coming in and out." It was the first time he called me his girlfriend.

One night, Reed and I were asleep when echoing voices from the street reached our breezy bedroom window. An argument was brewing below us on the sidewalk. Before my eyes could fully open, Reed was throwing on a pair of shoes and running down the fire escape — still shirtless — to defend his loyal landlord. I sat up, wearing just one of Reed's T-shirts and my underwear, climbed out of bed, and tiptoed through the dark apartment. The side door leading to the fire escape was left open, allowing the yellow glow of a streetlight to trickle through the living room. I followed Reed's path and peered down the stairs. Even in the middle of the night, the air was still warm and heavy.

The thing about Reed was, although I saw him as strange magic, he saw himself as nothing but darkness. He tried to cling to goodness in those around him, practical strangers easily winning him over, even those as fringe as a landlord. Reed could make you feel seen. Both Marley and I felt his very particular warm glow. He made sure to say how he felt, either through a lingering smile or a pencil crayon card. He wasn't a typical twenty-five-year-old boy; he was comfortable in his feelings, letting people know why they were special. They were rare qualities, and ones I tried to emulate. It was as if he hated what he had inside, so he would surround himself with light, before eventually destroying it.

Reed and I were becoming everything I hoped we could be. It was a fresh start. Nothing about our life together felt like it had the year before. We were closer, happier, more open. We spent that sweltering summer watching movies and drawing all over his bedroom walls. We sat on his bed, both in his T-shirts and grey briefs, drawing on each other's arms and listening to the Beatles, particularly "Don't Let Me Down."

"I was hurt that I had to hear from Ben you guys were moving," he told me one night after I brought up the hole in my door.

"You think I wanted to live next to you, bringing other girls home? Why would I want that?" It was still raw.

"I just wouldn't have bailed. I would have stayed and worked through it." He paused. "But I guess we're different people."

Reed drew four dots for his name on the crevasse of my hip, a spot that he loved. We made a symbol for our relationship — concentric circles like the inside of a tree — which we drew on each other's forearms and considered tattooing. Two aliens alone on our own planet, speaking our own language, figuring each other out. We were falling in love, and it felt like the serious kind. I didn't want to be anywhere that didn't feel like him. My loneliness left me alone if I was near Reed.

One afternoon, I found myself in need of tampons with no choice but to fight through the embarrassment and just tell him what was going on. He smiled and said, "I'll go for you. What do you need?" Not long before this, he was sneaking into my bedroom in the middle of the night as I pretended to sleep in matching pyjamas or underwear that didn't have holes. Back then, I didn't know what made him laugh, his favourite meal, or what kind of relationship he had with his family. We were only alone after dark. But now he was starting to feel like my safest place, and one of his best qualities was his ability to never make me feel shame or embarrassment about sex, periods, body hair, acne, nothing. He wasn't the type of boy who made you embarrassed about shaving your armpits or worried about getting blood on the sheets. He helped me download both Katy Perry and Foo Fighters. Reed liked the messiness of humans and had the gentle ability to make everything feel perfectly okay. In fact, the messier, the better.

These months revolved entirely around spending as much time together as possible. My eventual new restaurant job, errands, family, and friends were just little interruptions keeping me from Reed. I've never had any sort of drug addiction, but from what I've read, I imagine it feels a little bit the way this did — always looking to get my next fix without any control over my cravings. In the evenings, I checked my phone over and over waiting for that *knock knock* text. Then I'd sprint down the stairs to the back door of my apartment building. Skateboard in hand, he'd kiss my forehead, then we sat around all night listening to records and reading.

I was still hiding our rekindling relationship, and the shame of lying to my friends would occasionally sneak in, but his presence alone was enough to chase the anxiety away. My friends just didn't know how much I loved him, and how uneventful our days together really were. The mundane made it difficult to understand how anyone could be so opposed to us being together. We were normal. We loved each other. We weren't robbing banks; we were just complicated. Besides, it wasn't anyone's business. As Reed often reminded me, only we needed to understand our relationship. The hole kicked into my door, the other girls, the inconsistencies — that was then.

I also started to share more about my anxieties, more specifically, my fears surrounding food.

"I'm convinced I will get food poisoning if I eat at McDonald's or something."

"So, you've never had like . . . a Big Mac?" He asked me one sunny afternoon on my balcony.

"I've never had a Big Mac."

He laughed and said, "That's crazy!" I shrugged. "Okay, here's what we're gonna do. Tomorrow, we're going to McDonald's. There's one right around that corner, right? Okay, we're going to get two Big Macs. I'll eat it with you, and we'll face your anxiety together."

If anyone else had suggested this, I would have said no way in hell. But a flash of his teeth was all it took, and the next day I threw on my favourite pair of denim short shorts and we brought two Big Macs back to my balcony. He went first.

He told me, "There. Now if you get sick, I'll get sick, too." There was something and everything about him, so I took a couple bites.

He waited for my response. "Do you like it?"

"No!"

He ate the rest of my burger.

Reed was never bothered by the complexities of my mental health. He didn't mind that I was mostly sad and wasn't scared off by the cuts that sometimes lined my inner arms. While I made sure to hide them from most, Reed was one place I didn't have to. In fact, I knew he was doing the same thing in his own way. For him, it looked like drugs, sleepless nights, and disappearing. Our self-hatred and anxieties looked different, but he understood the world felt too heavy and watched as I buckled under the weight. We were both simply trying to cope. He coped through a desire to search, to understand how others managed minds as loud as his, to escape. I coped through self-harm, food restriction, and Reed.

Late one night, both on top of the sheets, my legs thrown over his, Reed and I lay facing each other.

"I love you." Reed's low voice said suddenly and quietly.

My stomach leapt into my throat, and I searched his green eyes for signs that I somehow misheard.

But I saw none.

I ran my fingers through his black hair. "I love you, too."

Our love wasn't warm and cozy. It also wasn't sleek or romantic with wine and gifts. Instead, we were raw, painful, young love. Messy, tattooed, and tattered, spilling out of rooms of vinyl records and scuffed paint.

Deep down, I knew this was a short-lived detour. My life outside of Reed was sparkly. I knew I was momentarily, and only momentarily, living as if I was a broken person losing themselves in someone perhaps even more broken. I knew eventually I'd be plucked out and tucked safely back into my bright world. But while my entire being ached, I drew close to the only one seeing the world with the same sadness. I was never afraid of the dark.

Will I ever be able to be with him and feel completely safe?

CHAPTER 7

Once Marley was home from camp, Reed and I ventured out of the shadows with our new relationship and made plans to see a concert with her and Ben. The heat was easing and crisp fall air was just beginning to sweep over the city, ushering in a new chapter for Reed and me. Like the last day of a warm vacation, reality loomed low.

I was eager for Marley to see what my summer was like as Reed's girlfriend. When I told her I'd been seeing him again, I braced myself for her anger and justified feelings of betrayal — hadn't we moved for a reason? Instead, she showed me nothing but compassion and more understanding than I deserved.

Marley told me, "I had a feeling this was happening." She sighed. "I can't lie, it worries me. You were miserable around him. I don't love it. But if you tell me it's been better, I believe you."

Two nineteen-year-olds doing their best to help each other through it all.

And now, I was keen to prove Reed and I were stable, and the Reed who kicked a hole in our front door was a thing of the past. Now, he was the guy who picked me up from work, texted me good morning, and traced the Big Dipper in my beauty marks.

That night was the first time our friends were going to see us together as a couple, in the wild. Marley agreed to meet at Reed's apartment before the concert. My stomach was alive with butterflies as we walked over together, obsessing over the possibility of it being a mistake. What if my suspicions were warranted and Marley didn't want me to be with him? What if she gave me an ultimatum? But my worries dissipated the moment we were all together again. We sat around Reed's living room, drinking and laughing, as if no time had passed. It was easy, and a reminder of why I loved him so much; he fit in perfectly with Marley and me. Next to Reed, Marley was free to be herself, and the spotlight followed her. I've always told Marley that her best and worst quality is her charisma. She's magnetic, she radiates joy, and everyone wants Marley to like them. But there's another side to the coin, and that is, her brightness can blind even her. She is quick to forgive and easy to forget, too kind to hold a grudge. Because it's simply who she is, Marley wanted to see the best in Reed, and she chose to believe me.

Throughout the night, I beamed with pride. Reed and I sat next to each other at the show. I leaned against his shoulder and he threw an arm around mine. Marley snapped pictures. I'd never been giddier. After the show, Reed went to another bar, Marley went to her boyfriend's, and I made my way home to bed.

The painful memory of seeing Reed with other girls was never far from my mind. It was in moments like these, when Reed was without me, it became clear how much I still didn't trust him. As I brushed my teeth, I reminded myself that I could function alone. It had always been when I felt most like myself. Still, my mind swirled with visions of Reed standing at the bar, cheap beer in hand, talking to a girl who'd just seen the same show. She was obviously cooler than me, knew more about the band, wouldn't care if he slept with other people. I worried I would never trust him, no matter how much rebuilding we did. We'd been so wrapped up in our cocoon that leaving it and venturing out into the world, facing our friends, facing strangers, felt like a violation of us. But I had to let go and choose to trust him.

Much later that night, there was a knock on my front door. In pyjama shorts, I hopped out of bed and opened it up to Reed's dark hair and even darker eyes. It was a different version of the person who spent the evening with his arm around me just hours before. This Reed was angry. That side of him was no surprise; I'd seen shades of it in the past. Plus, it was obvious just by looking at him. Even to an eye untrained to his specificities, Reed radiated complications, tortured by his own brain. If this was a night when those demons were trying to make an escape, I was going to be there to hopefully get a better sense of what it was that had its tentacles wrapped so tightly around him. Sometimes he was a stranger.

As Reed stood in my doorway, it became clear this wasn't just a drunk person. When I pressed, he told me he'd done some drugs. Whatever he did was giving him a weird look in his eye, and I did my best to get a read on what exactly I was up against. I was much more equipped than the year before.

"Are you okay?" I narrowed my eyes.

"Yep." He had a way of piling anger onto the smallest of words, making my stomach lurch.

"What's going on?" I asked.

"What's going on with *you*?" It was accusatory. "Hm?"

Reed's green eyes had the ability to turn black and soulless in a matter of seconds, and those were the eyes I was meeting for the first time. He was standing only a couple inches from my face, and I felt something growing between the two of us, momentum building. Whatever it was, it felt poisonous. His body was seething, the air thick.

With no knowledge of where it came from, I suddenly heard my own voice ask, "Are you going to hit me?" The question came out of my mouth involuntarily, and yet, it caused the corner of Reed's lip to twitch as if it was the very thing he had been hoping to hear.

Without hesitation, he responded, "Do you want me to hit you?"

I wasn't sure what we were really saying. We stared at each other for a moment longer — the hallway of my building silent — and then he hit me. Across the face. It wasn't hard, which left me confused. *Was that a joke? Maybe he's just high.* I felt a switch in my brain, and in the quickest flash, the world around me blurred, and my body turned soft. Before I could make another move, Reed leapt forward, grabbed me by my upper arms, and threw me backwards. Holding me tight, we flew back through the front door, past the front hallway and into my bedroom where he tossed me backwards like a doll and pinned me down on top of my bed. In mere seconds, I was lying on my back, his heavy body on top of mine and his hand pressed tightly over my mouth. I struggled under his weight.

Although it probably wasn't long that I lay squirming under his familiar body, a place I'd been many times before, my mind raced with mounting panic. I tried to think: *Is Marley home? Is she coming home? Is she about to walk in on this? How can I possibly explain what's happening.* I was confused. I hadn't done anything wrong, at least not that I could think of. I focused on his strong hand pressed over my mouth. *Is he trying to stop me from screaming? Is he about to do something worse?* Reed stared down at me inches from my face with a look of disgust and rage in his eyes. I was in my own house, on my own bed, in the place I should have been safest, but I was terrified. My space, my home, had been invaded. How could I be looking up at my own ceiling, my own curtains, lying on the sheets my mom bought me, with a hand pressed over my mouth? My mom needed to stay out of this. I made sure not to think about her for too long.

The world around me had nearly frozen, but my mind raced.

Then I heard a tiny whisper, a faint nudge. My brain scanned deep in the back of my memories for one specific file; one I pretended not to notice for months, unless I'd had a couple drinks. It was from that night months before, after that hot shower when he hugged me so tight and told me he was sorry. That night we sat on my bed. He wrapped his hands around my shoulders and pulled me down just a little bit too hard. As I lay with his anger crushing my lungs, I had the sobering realization that maybe I wasn't actually surprised at all. Maybe he showed me exactly who he was months before he hit me across the face and pinned me to the bed.

The next thing I remember, I'm alone in my room.

An enormity hung in the air. Just one hour earlier, I was nineteen, obsessed with my boyfriend, drinking raspberry wine, and skipping through the city with my best friend. Now I sat alone in the dark feeling the plates shifting beneath me, nauseous at the thought of having been proved entirely wrong and yet entirely right. The rearview mirror showed me Reed, I just didn't want to accept it. I saw the damage done to my door when he learned I was moving. I felt his hands grip my shoulders.

I wondered if his actions were the drug's doing. Maybe he'd wake up full of regret, falling all over himself to apologize.

The sun rose just as it always did, but this time my arms were lined with tender light blue fingerprints. The memory of the night before was already tucked deep into the back corner, collecting dust. I was stunned and yet entirely unsurprised. Scared and yet completely unbothered. I couldn't tell Marley — she'd just agreed to give him a second chance.

I don't remember seeing Reed for the first time after that night, only that he looked different. Sounded different. The darkness that always hovered, the unease he always brought, they left my stomach fluttering in a new way. I remember feeling indescribably lost, not knowing what to do, or if my version of Reed was gone and life was now irreversibly different.

A new, very specific pit now lay dormant in my stomach, leaving me feeling sick, wrong, and somehow used. Like my old life was just that, distant and foggy. This was Day One. I remember everything was a first; the first time he touched me post-abuse, the first time I slept next to him post-abuse, the first time I told him I loved him post-abuse.

I remember when we did see each other again, I looked closely for flickers of remorse but saw none.

From that first blatant act of violence, a precedent was set: Reed and I did not discuss it. There are many aspects of this relationship that I try to make sense of now, and somewhere near the top of that list is understanding how I could possibly have kept quiet. I believe I knew, even in those early days, a discussion would get me nowhere. Reed would never acknowledge his devastating faults.

Instead, a mess of confusion engulfed me. I was unable to understand how I could possibly move forward when a big piece of me had so recently, and secretly, died. This idea I had of my life, a life that didn't include fear or violence, was no longer true. I questioned my sense of safety, my capacity to make decisions, my ability to choose right. Guilt tortured me with reminders that I'd gotten out once already but chose to bring him back in.

I'd met a monster and that monster knew my life — where I slept, and the streets I took home. Not only had I allowed him into my life, but I'd allowed him into the lives of my friends, too. He knew their addresses, the names of their siblings.

I'd also broken the unspoken family pact to never make such a catastrophic mistake. I'd grown up with a healthy example. I knew better than this, but now the ball had been violently dropped for all of us. My bad decision would reflect badly on my family who had always been the "perfect" one, with "the best kids," that somehow "just got it right." Now, because of me, there was a crack in our foundation, one I feared would be visible to everyone.

That was the worst part — carrying his actions like my own mistake.

Telling my family wasn't an option. I could never muster enough courage to break my parents' hearts like this, not when I didn't absolutely have to, and I didn't have to. All my parents could do was help me get away from Reed once again, like they did when we believed he was just a boy I liked who seemed to like his options. They'd swoop in and remove me from the situation before it could get worse. Through tears, I'd pack up my bedroom and find myself alone in the country. I couldn't be alone, without Reed, without Marley. My parents couldn't know.

The only way forward was to ignore it all. To tell no one and bury it. It would be a secret kept to myself — a heavy burden carried by no one but me. I wouldn't disrupt my parents' lives, I wouldn't shatter their hearts, and I wouldn't label myself the troubled one. All I could do was play the role of normal and maybe forget it ever happened.

Shortly after, I got an opportunity to do just that when Reed texted me. *Do you want to come with me to my dad's this weekend?*

This was surprising coming from a guy who kept everyone at arm's length, never initiating conversations or asking questions. He had a flip phone and was rarely the one to make plans.

Reed's dad picked us up from the city. I was eager but nervous to meet his father and study the person who created and raised this mystery. Reed loved his father deeply, and yet, I was never able to picture him as a son.

Pulling into their driveway, I was struck by its normalcy. They had a nice, typical home with a manicured yard. The house was fairly large, neat and so *normal.* The juxtaposition of these mostly beige rooms to Reed's bright blue city walls where creatures crawled threw my mind for a loop.

We brought our bags to the cool basement where Reed's dad had made up the pull-out couch. I gestured toward a photograph of an eerie, foggy forest, hung over the fireplace. "Did you take that?"

He said, "Yeah, in high school," as he unzipped his backpack.

"So, you've always been good," I said, examining the photo.

"I've always been something."

It was the only sign of Reed's eccentric mind in his father's conventional home. That day we let Dex play in the back yard, watched TV with Reed's dad, and I got to know his younger brother a little bit. He, like Reed, was cool: black hair, tattoos and a love of music. But he was less odd than Reed, a slightly muted version who easily fit in.

Later that night, Reed was going to meet a few friends at a rehearsal space.

"Don't go," his brother warned me in a way that made me feel accepted and understood. "It's dirty and fucking gross there." Reed smiled knowingly.

I began to feel embers of a newfound comfort and trust doing their best to stay lit. Something about knowing where he came from eased my mind just a little bit, as I was dealing with someone so radically unpredictable. In the light of Reed's childhood home, parts of the monster seemed to have vanished, chased away by laughter and the familiarity of family. My body, on the other hand, was much harder to convince. My stomach remained tense, seeing through the weekend for what it was: regular life, nothing grand enough to soothe the immense pain. I searched the eyes of his family for any sign they really knew Reed and the mask he wore. If they could sense he was slowly destroying my sense of self. I wondered if they knew and turned a blind eye, because after all, he was their blood. I swayed between compassion and disgust, understanding and judgment. Reed's father appeared gentle and kind. He seemed benevolent and really loved his kids. I wondered if he lay awake at night knowing in his gut that his son hurt the women he loved, wondering what poisoned him, or if he would never believe it. How could he? How could he ever picture his child, who he held as a smiling baby, pinning his girlfriend to the bed, covering her mouth? How could he believe such a duality existed in his son without ever seeing it with his own eyes?

Reed and I went for a drive around the town where he grew up. It was my first time seeing him drive and there was something about it. Isn't there always? Windows down, one hand on the wheel. We played Brand New's *Deja Entendu*, and I felt like I was sixteen again, sitting next to the boy I liked. Only now, the boy was twenty-five, we were driving around town just the two of us, and no one knew where to find me.

Do I do what I want to do, or what everyone else wants me to do? We're just young and in love!

CHAPTER 8

I now believe certain people are brought into our lives for a reason.

I met Blake on one of my first days at school studying media production. She previously studied textiles before switching majors. I'd just switched universities. Blake was unlike anyone I'd ever met, and from the moment I saw her, I was fascinated. She had long, jet-black hair, icy-blue eyes, and a low, smoky voice. Every day, B would march into class with unflappable confidence wearing a head-to-toe black gothic outfit. She had a nose ring, and wore heeled Dr. Martens and leather pants. One day she showed up to class in a crop top that said *send nudes*, belly button ring prominent. In theory, she was terrifying. But the moment we started talking, I was struck by her kindness and warmth. She was smiley and bubbly, a fascinating and unique contrast to her hardened exterior (but don't be fooled, she'll kick your ass).

Although we were only a couple of years older than our classmates, we felt miles away. They were living in residences and going out to campus bars. We lived downtown and our lives existed entirely off campus. Blake and I quickly became close friends in class, and one day as we were leaving school, she asked where I was headed.

I told her, "I'm just going home."

"Where do you live?"

I told her the intersection.

"No way — what building? Logan, my boyfriend, lives in that area. I'm heading over there, too, I'll walk with you," she said in her signature rasp. I told her my address and she lit up, "Stop. That's his building!"

That day as we walked home, Blake and I got to know each other a little bit more and she invited me to come up to her boyfriend's apartment and hang out with them some time.

She told me, "Next time we have a party or something, you should come. I'll text you. Bring your boyfriend."

Cameron was another new classmate of mine, an aspiring music producer with spacers, tattoos, and a leather jacket. He was sweet, slightly unsure, and thirsty for approval, as much as he tried to conceal it with piercings and messy hair. I never batted an eye at Cameron. With Reed around, everyone else felt young and tedious.

In one of our classes, Cameron and I were assigned into a group project. I winced a bit when I heard our names called out one after the other. In my life, this small ripple could easily become a tidal wave.

Later that week, I was in Reed's bright blue bedroom. We sat as we always did, me at the head of the bed, knees up, my back against the wall. Reed at the foot of the bed, bare feet flat on the ground, surfing his laptop. I watched the back of his head, occasionally taking off his hat to run his hands through his thick hair. We were comfortable in our shared silences, long past the early months when every moment screamed to be filled. I was happy just to be swallowed up by his world. He eased the pain of my brain.

I was still struggling to trust him. I couldn't stop my eyes from scouring the bedroom for signs of his infidelity. I hesitantly peered over the side of his bed, between the mattress and the wall, searching for proof another girl had spent the night. My stomach filled with dread each time I moved the blankets or glanced into the garbage can. I really lost my mind the time I found a blonde hair. I didn't say anything. I told myself: *Stuff comes inside from outside*. Bringing it up would only push him away just a couple more inches. How closely could I monitor my boyfriend before he decided I wasn't worth the loss of all freedom? How crazy had I become, and when had I lost every ounce of my confidence?

That particular afternoon, Reed and I were in a good place. We'd been more stable — relatively speaking — with no sizeable incidents for a few weeks, though the memory of his heavy body on top of mine was never far from my thoughts. Every night I climbed into bed next to him or he told me he loved me, my brain would flash to that night. The confusion of what he did grew every day, slowly taking up more space inside of me, pushing on my ribs, constricting my breaths. I'd bury my face deeper into the warmth of his neck and do my best to push it back down. If I didn't let myself think about it, it didn't have to impact our present. It didn't have to be *us*. And yet, even as I did my best to forget, it was ever-present, relentlessly weighing on my upper back.

I got a text from Cameron. *Hey, hey! We should get started on the assignment. When can you meet?* I responded, *Hey! Yeah, we should. Do you have time to get started on some research first*? One minute later, Cameron texted back, *Anything for you*.

I glanced up at Reed still at edge of the bed and deleted the conversation from my phone. This was just how Cameron talked, but Reed wouldn't see it that way, and I knew what it could mean. Although it had been a few weeks since Reed scared me that night, there'd been countless disappearances spurred on by various things he didn't like. Some lasting four days. Reed weaponized his disappearances — they were strategic punishments. Painful and cutting. It felt as though he looked for reasons to punish me and this text from Cameron would fit his flexible criteria perfectly.

I closed my laptop and stood up from the bed.

"Where you goin'?" He asked, without looking up from his screen.

"I'm gonna shower quickly. I have class in about . . . an hour."

"I'll walk with you, if you want," Reed said as I undressed.

"That's nice. Thanks. We need to leave in thirty," I closed the bathroom door behind me.

But a few minutes later, I was met with a completely different version of my boyfriend. Immediately sensing the air had frozen over, through mounting panic and still in a towel, I asked Reed, "What's wrong?" But he shrugged me off. Although I was used to his unpredictable, taxing moods, it still always hurt and painted everything just a little bit darker.

Soon after, we made our way down the fire escape.

It took a block of walking in silence until finally, eyes still focused forward and expressionless, he said, "So what's going on with you and this Cameron guy?" His voice was vaguely amused, proud of the trap he'd so gleefully laid out in front of me. A sharp zap ran through my every nerve.

"What are you talking about?" I tried to play it off, but the blood had already left my face.

Reed spun around on his heels. I stood frozen. I had class, it was my first semester, and I was still new. But if I let him go now, he'd most likely disappear and turn his phone off, which always sent me into a self-harming spiral landing me at my therapist's office with fresh damage hidden under my sleeve. I didn't know where he went on those days, but I had a feeling I wouldn't like it. So, I went after him. A choice that put him ahead of my class, my life, and myself.

I followed Reed back up the fire escape, and as the door closed on the sunny day outside, a veil of darkness fell over us both. Once safely out of view, he said, "You deleted the conversation from your phone."

"You went through my phone?" I shot back.

"Why did you delete it?" He pressed, tone intensifying.

"Why are you looking through my phone?" I snapped.

He took two angry steps toward me.

This time, he wrapped both hands around my throat and launched his body forward, throwing me backwards by my neck in the apartment's small hallway. I flew into the wall, hitting the back of my head on the edge of the moulding of his bedroom door. Pain shot down my neck, and I struggled to think. Reed held me still, hands grasping my throat, with eyes full of rage. Reed was now an unrecognizable version of the person I slept next to, the one who drew me cards with hidden messages, the one I once trusted with my body. With one toss of that body, I was inside of Reed's apartment with a stranger. A stranger who had me by the neck.

I wanted to run into the bedroom and close the door, where no one could see us for what we really were. We were alone, but still, being thrown around in the middle of the apartment felt wrong. We weren't behind our closed door, guarding the secret. We had something big to hide.

There was no escaping it now. There were no excuses left to make: I was in a dangerous relationship. And this time, I was also in physical pain. Immediately after hitting the wall, the back of my skull began to throb. I thought my head had most likely split open.

Pressure mounted to my brain as Reed held my throat. When Reed finally released his grasp, I grazed the back of my head and checked my fingertips for blood. Thankfully, there was no blood, just the pulse of my racing heart pounding up the back of my skull.

I looked him in the eye and said, "Why did you just do that? Do you think that's okay? You cannot do that, Reed. I don't deserve this."

I don't remember him saying much at all.

As my body began to ache and my heart began to slow, I still had no intention of leaving him. The thought never entered my mind. If anything, I felt as though the handcuffs had just been tightened a little bit more. The more complicated it got, the tougher it was to walk away. In my experience, whether they're good complications like a shared apartment, shared history, and shared love, or bad complications like these dark secrets, the more complicated it is, the more unfathomable it is to leave it behind. In that moment, I never considered leaving him, nor did I want to.

It's a difficult thing for me to understand now, and yet, I recognize that girl and her choices. Profoundly confused, she was beginning to lose hope.

Soon after releasing me, Reed picked me up in his arms, took a few steps to the corner of his bedroom and lay me down gently onto his bed as if I was fractured glass. He disappeared to the kitchen and returned a moment later with an ice pack. Placing both hands behind my head, he gently guided it back down onto the cold sting of ice. I lay in shock, overwhelmed by the magnitude of what just happened. The back of my head throbbed, and I heard nothing but the sounds of my own breaths. I felt the need to quiet them, as if any sound made the moment real. Made us real, this day real, the suffocating reality of our relationship real.

I texted Blake: *I'm not coming in today. Not feeling good. Can you let me know what I miss?* And skipped the rest of my classes, too shaken to focus and too consumed by Reed and me to leave us, even for a few hours. Inexplicably, the desire to stay close to him was overpowering. He shattered me and now he was the only one capable of fixing me. No one outside of Reed could bring me back to life because only he knew the truth, rendering anyone else empty and useless. The one thing worse than the bleak realization he would most likely do it again would be having to face that thought on my own. Instead, I stayed in the false safety of his bedroom, cocooned in this world only we knew existed.

The next day, Reed gave me a handmade card and a present from my favourite clothing store. "I know I can be a difficult asshole," he said as I wrapped myself in his blankets, my body instinctively shielding itself. "I love you. You are all that is good in the world. I just forget it sometimes." He told me, eyes glued to mine. I hoped for the promise that it would never happen again, but it didn't come. Maybe he knew it was one he couldn't keep.

Although his actions screamed that I deserved to be punished, that his anger was warranted, I could still see a misty outline of my true self through his thick fog of rage. Reed's behaviour was a reflection of him and his demons, not my mistakes. Deleted text messages didn't warrant hands around my throat, so an apology would never leave my lips. Not after that.

Still, I relished being treated like porcelain even if it only came after being carelessly thrown around like rubber. Reed rarely took care of me like this, rarely made me feel like I was something to be protected. Suddenly, I held the power. For a brief time, I didn't fear him disappearing; he was trying to hold me tight. It was now that I felt most loved. How could I possibly consider leaving?

My knowledge of domestic violence highlighted broken bones and black eyes. I thought of dangerous men as large, angry, loud, and violent, screaming insults and insecurities. I imagined victims crying and fearful, but I had yet to shed a tear in front of him. It was somehow lost on me that this quiet, artistic, trusted lone wolf was hurting me in the same way as those who suffered black eyes. Because these things escalate. And one thing was clear to me even then — things were escalating.

But what do I do if I prefer to be sad with you?

CHAPTER 9

The level of entanglement I had with my abuser was mild compared to many other women's realities, like those who are married with children and whose husband of twenty years is violent. Reed didn't control my finances, my access to a car or cell phone. I had places to turn and family with money. I was relatively shackle-free, in theory, yet even I felt trapped in this world I believed I'd cultivated for myself. It's an isolating, chilling feeling; the moment you realize you're marooned with someone you love, and he's also capable of throwing your body against a wall.

It was late November, just over a year since we'd met, and now, I could hardly recognize either of us. He was a whole different person to me. Once again, I'd asked my parents to bring me home to the country, to hide. That day, I was confident in my ability to end the relationship. I'd opened up to Marley and hinted he was controlling and maybe even emotionally abusive, though never using those terms specifically. I'm not sure if I was in denial or simply didn't have the language. Probably both. My mind rarely went anywhere as serious and heavy as "abuse," instead, he was just difficult. Distant. Depressed.

"I never feel like we're on solid ground. He'll get mad and disappear or make me feel like I'm constantly doing something wrong," I skirted around the truth. "If we're having a good day, I'm so happy. Happier than I ever thought I would be. But it doesn't last. Honestly, he may just vanish entirely one day. I wouldn't be surprised."

"It all seems volatile and codependent," she told me. I had no idea what codependent meant. "Plus, it isn't helping your mental health. I just see you slipping backwards. He isn't healthy, Cal."

"I don't know how to not be with him, though. He's become this big thing, this person. I don't know how to be without him. It's like I'm losing my mind." What I didn't say was that I'd been slapped across the face and thrown through the apartment. "I don't *want* to be without him."

Marley came with me to my parents', which was, in part, because I couldn't bear to face them alone. I worried if my mom looked into my eyes she'd see what I'd seen. My parents were watching me deteriorate, collapsing into myself more with each month that passed, without explanation.

The memory of this conversation is fuzzy and confused. Some of it feels like a dream.

Next to Marley, I sat balancing on a stool at the kitchen island. My hands folded gently on my lap, my shoulders hung forward, weighed down by shame and exhaustion. I knew expectant eyes were focused on me, waiting for mine to finally look up and meet theirs. My parents and sister stood across the room.

"What happened?" My mom's voice broke the silence. My stomach leapt. I stared down at my hands and picked at a hangnail. Pick. Pick. Pick. Stop. Pick. Pick. Pick. I knew the longer I waited to answer, the worse their imaginations would be. Pick. Pick.

"What happened, Callie?" My mom tried again. I felt my eyelids sink so heavy that my entire face was being pulled to the ground. It would have taken all my strength to speak, to smile, to ever laugh again.

"Did he hit you?" There, someone said it. Pick. My eyes filled with big, wet tears and finally, I looked up. All I could muster up was a small nod, the tiniest confirmation of their greatest fears.

"What?" My little sister's voice said to my right. I glanced at her. Just a teenager, she looked panicked and terrified.

That's all I remember from the one and only time I admitted to my family I was being abused, and it was before the worst of it even happened.

The next day, Reed began calling me over and over. I turned my cell phone off. I didn't want to be tempted into talking to him. I had to quit. Admittedly, part of me was enjoying the comforts of the driver's seat. There were many days I spent trying to piece together what I'd done to make him disappear, calling him, replaying the day before in my mind, searching for the moment in his eyes when I pissed him off in just the right way. I'd walked to his apartment countless times, but he wouldn't answer the door. This time, he was looking for me. For once, I had some control. It felt terrible and so good.

I was sitting on my parents' bed with Marley when I turned my phone back on to see if I missed a message from anyone else. I had a text from a close friend telling me Reed showed up at her apartment, knocked, and covered the peephole (a tactic he'd used with me). She didn't answer. He also called and messaged her, asking if she knew where I was. Marley left the room, and next to me, her BlackBerry rang. I answered.

"Hello?"

"Hey. Where are you? I've been trying to call you. We need to talk." It was a familiar voice. I hung up and glanced at Marley's missed calls. Reed had been calling her over and over and over and over again. All day. I knew I shouldn't have answered his latest call, but I'd lost control. I needed a taste of his desperation; it was not the indifference I could recite. The only Reed I knew was distant and withholding, doing anything to push me off-balance, to keep me fragile and dependent. Knowing he was desperately trying to find me was almost intoxicating, a shred of evidence that he did love me and didn't want to lose me, which was all I'd ever wanted to hear. How was I ever expected to resist?

"Why did you answer that?" Marley grabbed her phone from my hand and looked at me with worried eyes.

"I don't know. I don't know. I just needed to talk to him." I didn't understand myself.

"You can't, you're just going to fall right back into it," Marley said. "I know him, and I know how persuasive he is." We stared at each other.

"What am I going to do?" I searched Marley's face for help.

"You just can't talk to him right now. You aren't far away enough from it, and you'll fall right back into your pattern. He's so bad for you. I think you have to just cut him off until you're stronger." Marley sounded sure, and I needed the direction.

I sent Reed an email letting him know I was not in the city, and I thought it would be best if we didn't speak anymore. He needed to know he wasn't going to find me, hopefully stopping him from showing up at any more front doors, which was equally concerning and embarrassing. The knot in my stomach twisted knowing I'd potentially put one of my friends in danger. She lived alone. He responded, first asking me to come back to the city and talk to him, and then saying that he would never end things with me this way and that I owed him a conversation. When I didn't budge, he wrote me again saying I'd helped him with his substance abuse and he'd practically given everything up since we got back together.

He also said he'd been sad, and now, without me around, he'd have *no one to take it out on.*

My selfish, destructive mind knew that by involving my friends, they could now hold me accountable for ending the relationship, a thought which terrified me. I couldn't hide what our relationship had become if he directly involved them in our drama and toxicity. I couldn't go back to him if my friends were reminding me of our volatility based on first-hand experience. I had to put out the fire, let the smoke clear, and wait for my friends to be consumed by their own lives once again. Then I'd reevaluate.

What I didn't realize was that I'd just tried to leave.

Leave.

A word that carries so much.

Hope. Fear. Judgment.

Why didn't you just leave?

A lot of us know the name Gabby Petito. Gabby was a twenty-two-year-old American and aspiring vlogger, killed by her fiancé, Brian Laundrie, during a cross-country van trip. It was a case closely followed across social media in real time. We then learned even more grisly details in the 2025 Netflix documentary *American Murder: Gabby Petito.*

On August 12, 2021, during their van trip, Gabby and Brian were pulled over and questioned by police after they'd received a call to report a domestic dispute stating, "The gentleman was slapping the girl." As we saw from police body-cam footage, Gabby was in a very different state than Brian. She was crying, anxious, asked to call her mom and, most notably to me, seemed to downplay the incident, which had led to a scratch on her face, saying, "He grabbed my face, I guess. He didn't, like, hit me in the face. He didn't like punch me in the face or anything." With every answer Gabby gave the police, it seemed to me as though she was trying to protect Brian.

Then the officers spoke to Brian, and the contrast was striking. Brian framed himself as the good guy who did nothing but try to de-escalate. Gabby was the problem. "She gets really worked up and when she does, she swings, and she had her cell phone in her hand so I was just trying to push her away." Brian's retelling seemed to have worked. The officer stumbles and says "In no way shape or form, from what I can perceive, does what happened here, a little slap fight between fiancés who love each other and want to be together, can I perceive that this is going to digress into a situation where he's going to be a battered man."

The police chose to separate the couple for the night, instructing them not to communicate. Brian was brought to a nearby motel, Gabby left to spend the night alone in the van.

Gabby went missing a few weeks later, and Brian was found to be hiding out at his parents' house (with Gabby's van in the driveway) refusing to cooperate with police or speak to Gabby's parents.

Eventually, after immense speculation and a social media spotlight on the case, Gabby's remains were discovered in a Wyoming national forest on September 19. She died by strangulation.

Brian Laundrie later took his own life, claiming in a notebook found near his remains that Gabby had fallen into freezing cold water, and was in so much pain that he murdered her, saying it was "merciful."

Between the body-cam footage, subsequent released texts between Gabby and Brian, unused footage from Gabby's vlogs, and a letter discovered from Gabby to Brian, it is obvious Brian was an abuser.

In an effort to share Gabby's story and highlight the signs of domestic violence, Gabby's family took part in a Netflix documentary about Gabby's murder, which came out in February 2025, four years after her death. The final scene of the documentary shows Gabby smiling and happy, running free on a beautiful sandy beach on a sunny day. The song that plays, "Take My Hand" by Matt Berry, sparked something interesting on social media. To the same song, women began posting about their experiences with domestic violence and, in honour of Gabby's memory, the importance of leaving.

One video shows photos of a woman's own bruised, swollen eyes with the words *she left,* followed by clips of her dancing with friends, smiling, living, and the words *so she could live.*

Here is a sample of some thoughts shared by women to "Take My Hand" in honour of Gabby's story:

> *If I didn't leave after he strangled me, I don't think I'd ever be able to witness another beautiful sunset again. Leave.*
>
> *Watched the Gabby Petito documentary and [bawled] my eyes out remembering I'm one of the lucky ones who made it out of an abusive relationship alive (barely) but so many women aren't as lucky. Just a reminder that if he hits you, he can kill you. It. Will. Only. Get. Worse.*
>
> *Sometimes I start invalidating my own experience, but this documentary is such a good reminder. A man who yells, is physical and violent,* IS *capable of killing you. So glad I got out of that relationship and rooting for all the women who are still in it.*
>
> *I am so grateful I survived.*

That day at my parents' house was my first attempt at leaving.

Unfortunately, it didn't stick.

Life without Reed was dull and empty, my nerves accustomed to instability and constant unease. Without it, my days were colourless. I was deep into my addiction, something I couldn't see at the time. As soon as I was back in the city, I was back in the blue bedroom feeling equal parts disgusted and relieved. That's the thing about these relationships; they're painful and heavy, trapping, and worse than you could ever imagine. Yet, you begin to forget how to function without them. Eventually, no amount of healthy love could replace the high. I was happier being sad with Reed than safe without him.

Back then, I didn't know most women go back before they finally get out. Multiple times. I didn't understand the magnitude of trying to leave. In my mind, it was an unstable, immature relationship that broke up, fell back together, broke up again, and fell back together. My youth and inexperience stopped me from seeing the truth of the excruciating pattern I'd just entered. I was up against much more than I was capable of admitting or even recognizing. These were complicated and nuanced experiences, and my brain was one of a nineteen-year-old who was just trying to survive it.

Not only was I in love with Reed and didn't want my relationship to end, but a piece of my very fabric was now made up of him. I couldn't possibly fathom existing without him near, without the tension he brought, without his complicated mind distracting me. I ceased to remember where I found joy before him or how I ever loved anyone else. He had rewired me entirely to depend on him for love, for thrills, and for happiness. Tearing myself away from Reed, even while knowing what he was doing was wrong, simply wasn't an option.

The rusty fire escape was sprinkled with snow, and the next day, I was leaving for California to spend Christmas under the desert sun. I showed up unannounced at Reed's front door with Christmas gifts, already anxious at the thought of being apart for two weeks. The year before, this very thing hadn't gone so well.

Reed and I exchanged gifts and soaked up our last few hours of each other. He gave me a Dave Grohl autograph and a handmade card. I'd finally found him ELO's *Time* on vinyl and a Daniel Johnston T-shirt like the one often worn by Kurt Cobain. The blue bedroom smelled like dusty radiator heat, and he felt like home. I loved our little life together. I tried to make sense of exchanging gifts and lying around, while also being acutely aware that things could change with something as simple as the closing of our bedroom door. Fear lingered just beneath the surface of every moment. Some part of me wondered how this man who loved me could bruise me. Part of me hoped for a couple of light blue marks to bring to California; a visual reminder of the secrets we were keeping — proof my confusion was both real and warranted, proof I wasn't imagining it all.

We spent only a couple hours together. I tucked myself under his arm with his hands in my hair. As we lay in bed listening to City and Colour and the Smiths, I asked, treading lightly, "So, have you made an appointment with a therapist yet?"

"No, but I found a few names. I'll call them." It was enough to get me off his back, at least for a little while.

"Do you know what you're going to say?" With my head on his chest, my muscles tensed.

"Not really. I guess just that sometimes I don't cope well with . . ." He trailed off.

Reed agreed to find a therapist and attend at least a couple of sessions to address his behaviour. At least, that was my understanding. To the best of my recollection, the conversation that got us to that point didn't acknowledge the specifics of why I wanted him to go, nor did it confront that he was, in fact, abusive. But we both knew what was being said between the lines as we side-stepped over any heartbreaking words. Reed agreeing to see someone made me the most hopeful I'd been in a long time, perhaps the most hopeful I'd ever been. It was a step toward finally acknowledging what was happening in our relationship and seeking to correct it. Yet, I wondered, even if that did miraculously happen — if he put in the work and eventually began to heal — how many obstacles would I still have nailed to the ground in front of me? Life with a complicated man was going to be complicated. Full stop. His complications were going to hold me back forever. And even if the violence in our relationship did stop, it would always exist in my mind. It could never really end.

I never truly believed these types of men were capable of changing.

But I looked up at Reed and hugged his body tight.

Eventually, he walked me to my car and I was sick to my stomach at the thought of us being apart. A twisted separation anxiety was forming, like a messy, sticky spider web. I wanted to die, except when he winked at me.

"I don't want to leave you at all," I told him.

"I know. I don't want you to go, either. But it will go by fast." He leaned against my car and brushed the hair out of my face.

"Don't disappear on me, okay?"

"Don't worry, little girl. I'm not going anywhere. Plus, you're going to have a great time. I wish I was going to California."

"Yeah . . . But I get anxious when I'm away from you."

"I'm not going anywhere."

He promised to email me every day.

I hardly recognize myself in our emails. My strange language and lack of self-awareness, our obsession. We dance around the abuse, like one email in which I say he's too *aggressive* with me. We expose ourselves for being in too deep, feelings too heavy to be at all sustainable. I cling to any thread of evidence that he can love me in the most conventional ways, that he has the ability to treat me with kindness, and somehow find it within himself to acknowledge — and change — his violent tendencies. I send him longing emails, often playing into how sexual our relationship was, baiting him into admitting he needs me. For something.

Overall, there are good times, when we're pining to be reunited, and there are bad times, when I'm worried, and he's telling me the things I want to hear. Or blaming me. Then there are the normal emails. The ones that show how much we had in common, and how much we liked each other (something Marley reminds me of when I begin to question how I ever let this happen). We ebbed and flowed, floated and drowned, faster than any healthy relationship should. We were made delirious by each other, our desires manifesting in opposing ways; his through sex, mine through a lust for us to be loving and, above all else, normal.

In one email, I ask how the appointment went. He tells me it went well, and he got lots of tips for managing stress. *Exercise, meditation, writing*. He tells me these were things he already knew but he needed the *reminder*. I wondered how he expertly framed his reasoning for being there if he walked away with stress management tips to exercise and journal.

I wrote back: *But would you ever get into things that have happened, what you do, or why you react certain ways?*

He wrote: *I know I need to, but I guess I'm easing into it. I want to feel comfortable before telling her about what has happened and about the aggressive side of our relationship. These appointments are going to be an ongoing thing. I'm working on it.*

They were not, in fact, an ongoing thing.

It's okay. Everyone makes mistakes. It's okay. I'm okay. It's okay.

CHAPTER 10

In the fifth grade, I became best friends with a girl named Heather. She was fun, sporty, and bold. But she also had a mean streak. As our friendship developed, I started to sense it more frequently. One day, she jokingly picked me up, and I fell back into a desk. The next morning, I woke up with a bruise the size of an apple on my thigh. Another day, we were outside at recess when she playfully shoved me out of the way during a game. I hit the brick wall and bit my lip. Yet, I found myself needing to keep up with her and earn her approval. Together, we froze someone out who had previously been my closest friend. It's something I think of often and still haunts my dreams, unsure of how I lost myself for that period of time. I knew it was wrong, and I didn't feel good about being mean. I finally realized Heather was nothing more than a bully after I'd been home sick for a few days and a classmate told me, "Just so you know, Heather says a bunch of bad stuff about you when you're away." A twelve-year-old hero.

I decided to distance myself from Heather, and the anxiety she was causing me. I was riddled with guilt over having ever chosen her over my loyal friends and my family. I cried every day, and eventually, I couldn't get out of my parents' bed. A grey cloud followed me closely, and I believed in my bones that I deserved it. I'd made the wrong choice, spent time with the wrong person, been cruel, and worst of all, chosen evenings with her over my family. I was in such a bad place that my parents began planning activities just so I had something to look forward to. This included my favourite thing, going to work with my dad. At the time, he was recording a radio program celebrating The Beatles voiced by Denny Doherty of the Mamas and the Papas. I sat at the recording console, feet dangling, reminded of life beyond school, beyond being a kid, and beyond making some of my first mistakes. They were heavy thoughts for a small girl.

My unrelenting guilt was accompanied by fear of regret and fear of making mistakes. The first time I felt real guilt, I was in first grade. Tamagotchis were the thing to have and therefore hard to come by. My mom stood in a long line at Toys "R" Us and came home with a blue and pink Tamagotchi. The next day, a fellow first grader offered to trade me for it. So, I did. I gave him my Tamagotchi and he gave me his red dinosaur knockoff. When I saw my mom in the playground at the end of the day, I felt like I'd committed a crime. I was sick to my stomach and couldn't look her in the eye. I knew she'd waited in line to buy it, and I'd given it away. I cried all night, counting the minutes until I could get back to school and negotiate the safe return of my precious Tamagotchi.

I carried that guilt for years. So much so that I still have that Tamagotchi today in my thirties. I had many of these moments growing up. The emotions were consuming and astronomical, and without the tools to cope, I shut down. In order to help me release the guilt I was carrying like bricks in a backpack, my mom took an empty Kleenex box and had me write *Callie's Regret Box* across the top. Every night I wrote down one of my regrets, folded up the little piece of paper and put it in the box. Once that regret was in the box, I was no longer allowed to worry about it, that particular burden had been released. *I regret not being nicer to my sisters today. I regret excluding someone at school. I regret hurting my mom's feelings.*

My regrets still lurk like eels in the coldest depths of personal disappointment. My shame eats me from the inside out, constantly torturing my thoughts. Decades after Heather and the regret box, I search for the reassuring words of strangers through vulnerable articles and revealing memoirs. I seek guidance to help me let go of my wrong decisions and heavy shame, which make me feel like vomiting.

I really thought I knew how it felt to beat myself up, then I met Reed.

Intimacy looked different for Reed and me. Different than I imagined, different than I'd seen on TV. This part of our relationship left me feeling wrong and guilty, just as I had all those years ago as a little girl who knew she was making the wrong choices.

Sex with Reed brought with it immense guilt and shame. They were difficult feelings to label, and even more difficult to truly understand their root cause, especially when sex was the very thing that made Reed happy and to an extent, made me happy, too. Reed used sex as a Band-Aid, as a drug, as entertainment. To him, it was everything. It didn't matter where we were, what we were doing, or whether he was angry with me, Reed wanted sex. Like the time I had an anxiety attack and called him. When he showed up, I was crying in bed and he tried to have sex with a coaxing, "Let me make you feel good." There was no time off from his constant pressure and my constant worry. It left my young, inexperienced mind paralyzed with confusion and left me occasionally hiding tears.

Reed and I didn't talk much about his violence, except occasionally in terms of our sex life, which became increasingly more intense as months passed. Maybe addressing it by way of sex made it feel less like I was unarmed and running straight at the angry elephant in the room. But the familiar weight of guilt had been quietly swirling for some time. So, one day, pushing through my hesitation to rock the boat and my fear of his irritation, I asked Reed to stop hitting me across the face during sex, something he started doing one day and after that, never stopped. The next time we had sex, he made sure to look me in the eye as his hand hit my cheek. I stopped him in the moment and said, "I asked you not to do that." He hit me again immediately. I gave up — that time. Reed continued to hit me whenever he wanted. Each time, my stomach would drop as I suddenly became acutely aware of how naked I was, no armour, no witnesses, no proof. My body, small next to his. Him, broader, stronger. I knew, even through my persistent self-doubt, he was reminding me he was in charge. I watched as his body overpowered mine.

Fear would have been an appropriate feeling, so why, instead, did I fill with shame? I knew this wasn't the way I deserved to be treated. I'd had other experiences, which hadn't left me with this same desire to curl up in a ball and cry on top of the kicked-off sheets.

Filled with dread but fuelled by anger, I found it in myself to bring it up with him yet again. This time I decided to be more direct. I said, "You hit me in real life, so you lost your right to do that during sex." I wasn't sure it even made sense, but it's what came out.

Reed looked at me, "I think you like them both." My toes curled.

By saying those words in broad daylight, I broke our unspoken pact and exposed the other side of us. Our dark, rotting underbelly. Reed and I had a silent agreement not to talk about the abuse. In the extremely rare occasions that I did allude to it, I skirted around the subject by saying things like "the way you treat me," careful never to use painful words like *hit* or *abusive.* That day was the closest I'd come to addressing the violence directly. But regardless of the boundaries I managed to choke out, it had no impact on Reed. He never stopped hitting me across the face. In fact, it just continued to progress.

Eventually, I developed a go-to line for just before sex. I asked, "Can I feel that you love me a little bit this time?" It was my way of hesitantly wading in and requesting that we not have angry sex, asking him to be gentle.

"That's no fun," he said, as he dug his teeth into my bottom lip. I somehow loved the smirk that flew across his face when he got his way.

If I wasn't fun anymore, he would find someone else.

And just minutes later, he'd wrap his hands around my throat, spit on my face, grab me tight enough to leave bruises, slap me, and place his lips against my ear and whisper, "Scream for me, bitch." I'd stare blankly at the ceiling, feeling my mind and body disconnect. Distance was the answer. Distance made it survivable. I let my mind wander — let myself momentarily forget who I was, where I was, the severity of it. Sometimes, I fought back tears. Other times, I leaned in, determined to keep it from being one-sided. If I was an active participant, it couldn't be wrong.

Right?

The best I got was minimally less aggression. Mostly, we had angry sex.

It was around this time I had a dream Reed was cutting my wrists. I smiled at him as he dragged a knife across my pale arm. His hands held me gently and I felt no pain. I woke up truly believing all I had to do was ask, especially after he had me bite hard enough to draw blood. Our love often looked like hate, and yet, I'd never loved so hard. I saw him as a drug; he saw me as a meal.

The shame of it all became unbearable in my quietest moments.

Alone in my apartment and staring into space, the heat of anxiety began inching its way up the back of my neck. I had the sickening feeling I was in way over my head. I was in love with him. Marley and I had chosen to weave our young, fun, nineteen-year-old lives tightly to his.

I flipped open my laptop, pulled up YouTube, and searched the only reference for abuse I could think of: Rihanna and Chris

Brown. Up popped an interview where Rihanna described Brown's violent outburst in the car on their way home from an industry event one evening. Chris Brown punched Rihanna in the face, held her in a headlock, and even bit her. I studied the way she described the attack, searching for familiar looks, words of warning, anything, to help make sense of the nausea rolling in my gut. The video showed photos of Rihanna's swollen, bruised face, and I thought to myself: *If this is abuse, then that's not what's happening to me. I've never had a black eye. My face has never been swollen. I've never called the police.*

At the time, black eyes were how I measured abuse. Those were the images I'd seen, the stories reaching the top of the headlines. Everything else was still lost on me. In the 2024 documentary *Marilyn Manson: Unmasked,* one of Manson's victims and *Game of Thrones* actress Esmé Bianco says Manson "would hide abuse by doing it during sex." This is a reality that took me years to face.

I could barely recognize the hollow person I'd become. The last year had poisoned every previously untouchable corner of my life. There was a time when I wasn't this haunted, lost person. Violence was never a part of my life. But now, my eyes saw nothing but hopelessness. I'd drifted miles away from everyone I once turned to for comfort, dodging calls from those who could normally read every twitch of my eyebrow, lost under the weight of shame. Feeling gross, stained. I didn't know me anymore.

I wanted Reed and his problems, this hadn't waned. But as I tried to decide which lines had truly been crossed, the loneliness ached deeper than I ever imagined possible. No one would understand what I'd allowed to happen to myself. Uncoupling my life from his would be impossible. He slept in my bed, his T-shirt was on my floor. And worst of all, I'd spent the last year defending him. It was me who'd taken him by the hand and pulled him into my life. I couldn't take it all back.

Defeated, I slid backwards on my bed. He wasn't there, and Marley wasn't home. It was a moment alone. But as I lay on my side, my arms ached. I checked for bruises. They were faint, but they were there — light-blueish outlines of gripping fingertips. I couldn't place when exactly I'd gotten them, but the ache had become familiar. A sunny day was buzzing with activity just on the other side of my bedroom window. Kids were laughing, skateboards were rolling over city sidewalks, dogs were barking. Distant car horns honked and downtown traffic buzzed. There was still life around me, and yet, mine had stopped. I typed the words: *How do you know if you're in an abusive relationship?*

Why don't we just disappear
into your dark, cold bedroom
together. No one will ever hear
my voice again. I won't have
to face the fact that you're
bad for me.

CHAPTER 11

It's easy to judge me for staying in this relationship. Frustrating, even. It's also easy to judge me for somehow still managing to love him as strongly as I did, even as my body began to feel less like home and more like prison. My most critical thoughts judged me, too, wondering how I could possibly allow these prime days to be carelessly wasted, spent navigating the most vile type of man — one capable of violence against women. But inside, a different version of myself was just learning to walk, one that didn't care whether Reed would be considered a "bad guy" by my friends, family, or even society. She no longer considered how it was objectively "wrong" to hit your girlfriend. It was the new normal. It was reality. And it's surprising just how quickly we adapt, forgetting how life used to be beautifully unremarkable.

It's easy to judge me for sometimes looking past the parts of our relationship that scared me. It's even easier to see Reed as just one thing; when certain lines are crossed, other facets vanish. But for those living through it, the extraordinary does not simply erase the ordinary. The violence somehow never blinded me to the small reasons the nineteen-year-old girl was infatuated with the dark-haired, sweet, mesmerizing twenty-five-year-old boy who spent his mornings stretching on a yoga mat in the living room. The one who loved animals and signed his emails *love your soul.* His guarded softness took months to uncover and seemed to be saved just for me.

Reed lived in striped shirts which slid perfectly over his protruding collar bones and black tattoos. His laughs were swallowed as he battled outward happiness, covering his front teeth and pronounced jawline, embarrassed to be seen smiling. But here's the secret: he did laugh. Often.

I loved his scuffed-up skate shoes that were never properly tied, and the red backpack he brought everywhere. Loving Reed meant being given a backstage pass to his vulnerability, his off-beat mind, his rare yet focused attention. It meant feeling chosen, knowing no one else was quite as inside of him as I was, knowing others had tried but most never bothered. But I had. And now, I lay in his bed, learning what intimacy could truly mean. What it actually felt like — fulfillment between two people who are aware of the other's complexities and complications but who still chose each other.

It's easy to judge me for holding onto the light in between the dark. I judge me. Or maybe I feel as though I should. And yet sometimes, instead of judgment or shame, I come back to it all with sickening fondness. Thinking back to that time where every smile, every kiss, every touch sent zaps through my entire body, unable to believe my luck because I was still learning. Being with Reed meant watching him check his emails shirtless in bed. It meant holding his hand through the thumb hole in his ratty black hoodie. It meant turning over in the middle of the night and finding us face to face, and just for a brief moment, feel his lips on mine, both smiling, only for us to roll back over and fall asleep, most of the time forgetting it even happened once the sun came up.

It's easy to judge me for loving Reed. But his darkness did our passion many favours. Reed led with curiosity. Throughout the day, he sent me things I might find interesting: old interviews with Dave Grohl, an article about the recording of *Sgt. Pepper*, a picture of a dog in a hat. He drew me chaotic little pieces of art, and I knew to examine every millimetre for hidden messages. *I love you*, hidden in the pencil crayon. He wore thin yarn bracelets around his bony wrists. He winked at me from across the room. He told me I was all that was good in the world. He wrestled with Dex. He ate healthy food. He was handsome. He saw no flaws on my body. Whatever you were thinking, he wanted to hear it. He valued weirdness. "It's the duality," was his explanation for everything. He liked to teach me things; he told me about myths behind obscure bands I didn't know or the effects of hallucinogens on the brain. He taught me about sex. His emails had punny subject lines.

Lord of the Ringos

Grohl's Poor Brain

Llama Del Rey

He once said that without me, he'd spend the rest of his life just trying to replace me.

It's easy to judge me for staying in this relationship — until you are me.

I can't take this again. I have to put my faith into him. I don't want anything bad to happen. I have to believe that I don't deserve bad things to happen to me.

CHAPTER 12

I found myself living a double life, sucking me dry of all my remaining energy. My new life demanded endless lies and hours spent sneaking around. Hiding my addiction became a finely honed skill, strategically "missing" calls, fabricating fast lies about where I was, conveniently not sharing stories involving Reed. These moments became frequent, so I started sharing less, reaching out less, calling home less, and talking less. The answer was to simply disappear.

When Marley's cousins came to stay with us one weekend, I hid out at Reed's apartment. She thought I was at school, working on a big project, when in reality, we were still deep in our cycle of Reed disappearing and me swearing this time I was done. But in keeping with our pattern, I'd quickly let him off the hook and was once again hiding in the blue bedroom.

My phone lit up with Marley's name. I let the call go unanswered then followed up with a text. *Sorry, what's up?* She responded, *We're going for crepes. Wanna come?* My stomach went empty and nauseous.

The old part of me wanted to be with Marley and her family. I wanted to be safe and lie-free. I wanted life to be simple again. I missed the innocence. Marley had no idea just how bad the situation had become, how lost I was. She was with her family, and she was safe. But I was stuck and lying about it — all the time. Lying to Marley had become so painful that I started to avoid her, and eventually, I was unable to face her at all. I believed I was disappointing her, but more than anything, I knew she was right. Instead of acknowledging it, I took the easy way out and built her up as an obstacle. Marley became the enemy, and I, resentful. It was too hard to admit she was only triggering because she was the one mirror I couldn't avoid. Marley knew me better than anyone. She was also the only other person who knew Reed almost as well as I did. She was with me the day we came home to our damaged front door. She saw me crying and, on all fours, scrubbing the walls after Reed smacked a drink out of my hand, splashing it all over our front hallway and Marley's bookcase. She saw me sit in my room with the lights off, hiding from the world, when Reed decided to disappear for five days. She saw me begin to hate myself more with each day he ignored my calls as I wandered around the city searching for him. Marley knew how strongly I blamed myself for Reed's disappearances and watched me punish myself for not being good enough to keep him. She supported me each time I told her this was the last time, that I was done chasing him, hoping this time he'd stay. She supported my vague promises to leave him. But we both knew the next day she would come home to a dark apartment.

I was removing myself from Marley's life when all she'd done was try to protect me. Without complaint, she attempted to pull me out of the dark spiral he dragged me into, and I punished her for it. I hated the person I was becoming. The bomb Reed detonated in my life continued to wreak havoc. I wasn't this person who chose the wrong people. I wanted to feel protected by someone — anyone. I wanted life to feel good again. But I was trapped, not only by Reed, but also by how strongly I didn't want to leave him. Erasing him was unimaginable, yet it was all I wanted. I missed my old life — I missed the warmth I used to get around my family, I missed Marley and I being inseparable, and I missed feeling clean and right. But over the two months Reed and I were apart, and those relationships were intact, my depression became the loudest voice.

My poisoned mind assured me I was faced with the decision to make myself happy by staying with him or make my friends and family happy by leaving him. I was angry at everyone who made it sound as though leaving him would be simple. They didn't have to sit in bed missing him, worried they may never love anyone else with the same intensity. They didn't have to pry themselves free from his tight grip. They didn't have to go through the grief. They didn't carry the threat of repercussions. Urging me to leave was easy when they weren't the ones who had to do the leaving. Plus, how would I even leave? Wouldn't I be in even more danger? Everyone around me was hurting, and I didn't know how to stop it.

The reality of our dead end occasionally took centre stage in my mind. Some days, dodging texts felt like it was just part of it — normal, monotonous — while other days, the bricks of lies weighed heavy. One of those particularly heavy days, I needed an escape. I'd just gotten home from Christmas in California and we decided to book a hotel room for New Year's Eve. The hotel was just ten minutes from our life, but any separation was like a little crack of the window.

The city was dark, cold, and wet. The hotel lobby was full of party-ready twenty-somethings: drunk, loud, and freshly legal. Cheap lobby chairs and vases of faux flowers made me uneasy. Everything about the hotel felt fake — fake excitement, fake downtowners, fake cleanliness. Suddenly I felt like I was visiting the dorm of a friend where everybody knew each other but me.

Through a contained shout, the concierge said, "I just need a credit card."

Reed's head spun around and he looked at me with expectant, dark eyes. But my parents paid my credit card bill. It was for Broadcast Journalism textbooks and dentist appointments, not hotel stays with my secret boyfriend.

"I can't put this on my credit card, my parents pay it. I can't," I said and braced myself for his reaction.

As with any reminder that my friends and family didn't want me to be with him, a flicker of rage flew silently across Reed's face, and he reluctantly reached for his wallet. I stood just behind him, disappearing into his shoulder and the little world we hoped to have all to ourselves that night.

The hotel room was small and the halls buzzed with constant door slams and chatty gatherings by the elevator. I took off my shoes and climbed up onto the plush bed, balancing on my knees and flipping through channels. I gave myself permission to let it all go. Just for one night, I would forget the lies that were closing in and that we had a secret.

Reed lifted his backpack onto the end of the bed and began to unpack. A change of clothes, some beer, my sugary, juvenile wine. Then he removed a very specific shiny black plastic bag and placed it on the mattress. I knew that plastic bag well. It followed us — apartment to apartment. My stomach sank when I saw it emerge on this particular night.

Our sex life had become increasingly murky. As he liked to remind me, he was there to "wreck" me, to "take away my innocence," to "defile" me. I wasn't necessarily against it, especially when he presented it as though he really wanted to open my eyes and let us experience these things together. He acted as though he was teaching me everything. I was a blank slate, naive to the world of sex, and what physical connection could really look like. I was his puddy, ready to be moulded.

Reed started with the basics, making sure to let me know that they were, in fact, just an introduction. From there, he continued to push me in directions I'd never been, expanding what would emerge from the black bag every few weeks. Any lines I tried to draw were slowly edged backwards, using guilt and pressure as his tools of choice. And although it felt wrong deep in my weary bones, being pushed by Reed meant being pushed closer to him and further from myself, which was exactly where I wanted to be — submerged into his twisty life and momentarily distracted from my own lack of desire to be alive.

It was also a place that could make me feel like throwing up.

But there was something about that bag. The moment I saw it, on any given day or night, it was as if a monstrous grey cloud suddenly drifted over the sun, and what was bright just moments before lost all its magic. It meant I would once again be pushed. It meant I would soon feel ashamed.

That New Year's Eve, brand new things emerged from the bag. Before I had a moment to understand or agree to what Reed had planned, he was wrapping a leather collar around my neck and I felt the weight of a leash being clipped to my throat.

That night still weighs heavily inside of me because sex had already felt unsafe between us for months, regardless of the plastic bag and its contents. Reed consistently had me in my most vulnerable state. I handed myself over to him, blurring the lines between my body and his, allowing him to say when for both of us. And yet, his hands weren't ones that protected me.

That night, which was miles outside of my experiences and comfort — or anything I personally wanted to do, and with someone I didn't trust to be treating me with respect — left me traumatized. Every cell filled with a bubbling humiliation. I wanted to melt into the mattress and disappear. I was backed into a bleak corner; what made him special was his darkness. If I began to question his most distinguishing quality, I'd be forced to confront how unsafe I felt overall and how broken we really were — forced to admit I needed to leave but felt I couldn't.

I don't use the word traumatized lightly, but the shame and embarrassment of that night are still alive and well, close enough to the surface that they can awaken at any moment.

The point seemed to be for me to submit, to feel small.

It took me years to stop avoiding that night and finally begin to unpack its baggage, which weighed on my sense of self. By no means do I think partaking in these things is wrong, but when put into context with the rest of our history, it was traumatizing. One day, Reed slapped me hard across my lower back after I told him I didn't want to have sex. The sound of his hand hitting my bare skin echoed through the apartment. I turned around to look at him, and he looked back at me with nothing but rage and disgust. I felt myself shrink just a little bit more, another part of me lost, never to be found again. Other times, he had sex with my body even after I'd tried to gently say no. (Occasionally, I still blame myself; was I not clear enough?) There were times when it felt inappropriate for us to have sex — like at my friend's house next to her mom's bedroom, as her dad lay in the hospital, dying — but he simply insisted. ("I'll be quick. Come on. I won't be able to sleep.") He frequently forced himself so far down my throat that I gagged, then he gripped the back of my head with his strong hand and held me in place, leaving me gagging as long as he wanted while I slapped the hand on the back of my skull, desperate to be released. I woke up abruptly one night to him straddling my face, forcing himself into my mouth, only to wake up the next morning and laugh off the fact that he didn't remember. I believe Reed watched as I did things he knew I didn't want to do, pushing me further than I wanted to be pushed, taking part in things I wasn't enjoying, things that made me feel gross, all the while telling me, "Good girl."

I tried to play along, like the time I showed up in lingerie as a surprise. The delight I expected was instead passive placating. I believe he would have been happier if I'd shown up in my high school uniform, as he'd mentioned a few times. I wondered if he wished I was even younger than I was.

When his hands touched my skin, my body was no longer my own.

In Sophie Gilbert's fascinating book, *Girl on Girl: How Pop Culture Turned a Generation of Women Against Themselves,* she writes, "One 2010 study of more than three hundred popular pornographic scenes found that 88 percent contained some kind of physical aggression, typically spanking, gagging, or slapping, with force overwhelmingly being meted out against women by men." This makes a particular stat published by the *New York Times* in 2024 even more alarming. It states, "On average, Americans first see online pornography at age 12, according to a 2023 survey of adolescents by Common Sense Media, and 73 percent of those aged 17 and under have seen it, a figure consistent with other research. Of those who watch pornography, whether intentionally or by stumbling into it accidentally, more than half reported seeing violence, including rape, choking, or someone in pain."

While I can't know for sure if porn was a contributing factor in my own relationship and the confusing things I experienced, I think about it often, leaving me both worried and feeling utterly helpless. Twelve years old is astonishingly young to first see porn, and that could mean a twenty-five-year-old man has, in theory, already been viewing violent sexual imagery for thirteen years. At what point does the violence he's ingesting become normalized?

Another alarming moment in Gilbert's *Girl on Girl* addresses a particularly gross comment by comedian Russell Brand (who, in 2025, went on to be charged with rape, sexual assault, and indecent assault). During a 2006 stand-up tour, Brand joked that he liked "them blow jobs, right, where it goes down their neck a little bit . . .

them blow jobs where mascara runs a little bit." The audience, of course, laughs along as Brand imitates a gagging sound.

Everything circles back to consent, but also, respect. Are the young, impressionable, twelve-year-old boys seeing women being respected? How will this shape their relationships to women when they become men?

Do "jokes" like this one from Russell Brand normalize and, therefore, prevent us from seeing the truth in our own lives, leaving us unsure how we feel, or better yet, how we *should* feel?

What happened that New Year's Eve wasn't something I remember agreeing to, nor did I see the specifics coming (just that he had a surprise, which I did know was sexual). And yet, I was cast as the lead and thrown on stage. I caught a glimpse of myself in the mirror and felt a part of myself die. That night got under my skin and made relationships, sex, intimacy, my naked body, everything, feel wrong (though at the time, I assured him the night had been perfect). In reality, I was left feeling gross and dirty, as if it's wrong to have ever been a child — far away from someone who has sisters, friends, aunts, parents.

I don't believe true consent can exist when violence is also present. How can you properly consent when you feel threatened?

Reed seemed to be free of morals, either that or, I felt he simply enjoyed pushing boundaries and had fun doing it. To him, ethics seemed to be mere suggestions, nothing more than a challenge, and I saw Reed bend the law more than a few times. The first was through his possession of various drugs. Then there were the other times. The slightly stranger ones. Like the day Reed and I were at his local grocery store grabbing cheese perogies, frozen pizzas, Mrs. Fields cookies, and fruit, as we always did. As we stood in the checkout line, Reed picked up one of the small items already sitting on the conveyer belt and tucked it into his pants. My head spun around, meeting his amused eyes. "Why?" I whispered, with pleading eyes. There was no reason for this. We could afford it. We were paying for many more items. Why did he feel the need to steal this one small thing? He didn't acknowledge my question.

My frustration grew with each beep of the scanner as I pictured my parents' faces. I do not steal. We do not steal. We do not break the law. My anger was directed more toward myself than him. *How can I be dating this person? How is this my life?*

As Reed and I stepped out of the grocery store, a man followed us closely. Reed, clocking him, took off ahead of me. As the man passed me, he said, "He knows what he did, right?"

I was too exhausted by Reed to protect him, nor did I feel he deserved it.

I sighed, "I don't know."

The man's pace quickened, and soon, he was jogging to catch up with Reed who had turned the corner, leaving me behind, heading back toward his apartment. I sped up, too.

Around the corner, Reed was pushed up against the wall by the man, held by the shoulders. I kept a safe distance, gripping the rest of our grocery bags. I couldn't believe what I was seeing — actual consequences for his actions — part of me felt vindicated.

"What are you doing? What's going on?" I didn't know what to say, if I should admit I knew what he'd done. Reed tossed me the keys to his apartment, landing just in front of my feet.

Reed told me, "Go home."

I did as I was told. Reed stealing wasn't my problem. I didn't want to be involved; nothing was further from who I was.

As I walked home, I replayed the last few minutes in my mind. Both Reed and I were wearing all black, both in leather jackets. I knew what we must have looked like from the outside: two troubled kids, angry at the world. Broken people who found each other, running around and stealing.

I let myself into Reed's dark apartment and put the groceries into creaky cabinets, checking my phone over and over again. When he hadn't shown up after another hour, I climbed into bed and put on a movie to distract myself. I wondered what I was in for, if he would eventually show up angry, and if I would be met with the sinister version of Reed I'd come to know. I wondered if I should leave and go back to my own apartment. Then my phone rang.

"Hey. What happened?" I asked him.

"Hey! It's fine. That fucking guy saw me take it and went fucking nuts. They brought me back to the store and called the cops. The cop made me sit there for a bit. It's fine, they let me go. No biggie. You hungry?" He was happy. Happier than I'd heard him in months. The joy in his voice was unfamiliar, like he was calling me with some great news, as if he'd somehow won.

They're two very different things — stealing from a grocery store for fun and pushing my sexual boundaries. But they're also somehow one and the same. Evidence this person who I was so intertwined with seemingly had no regard for what was right. No conscience. No remorse. He'll tell you himself. He had a way of justifying the worst of his actions, like he somehow deserved unlimited free passes because he was "misunderstood," an "alien." And I was a vessel to absorb his glaring insecurities, his compulsions, his desires — something he seemed to believe was acceptable.

I hate you for what you've done to me.

CHAPTER 13

Reed and I ate a lot of Indian food together. It was our favourite takeout on nights we chose to treat ourselves. Two orders of butter chicken, two sides of rice, naan, and veggie samosas.

My anxiety often manifests in a fear of food, piggybacking off the ever-present emetophobia (or fear of vomiting). Heavier meals sit in my stomach like a rock and my imagination turns tie-dye. I imagine what it would feel like to vomit it back up. I imagine the taste launching into my throat, the sound of my body heaving, my insides regurgitating all over the floor.

But Reed liked Indian food and I felt brave enough next to him. Wanting to spend time with Reed occasionally overshadowed some of my fears. You know that feeling when you have such a grossly big crush on someone that even the most mundane errands are exciting? It was like that (think Carrie and Berger shopping for shower curtains — and that guy was truly the worst).

Reed picked up dinner on his skateboard. We never ate at the table, instead, we sat cross-legged on top of his plaid comforter. That night, anxiety rose with each mouthful of rice. Tension grew vertically in my throat, my body buzzing and my heart starting to pound. I took a couple deep breaths and did my best to keep the fear bridled.

Usually, if I can manage to harness the panic in the first half hour or so, it won't evolve into a full attack. There is a certain point of no return so the beginning is key. I have to maintain control. My ability to do so vastly varies from day to day with seemingly no explanation. I'll know a bad day is coming if I wake up with butterflies and the immediate weight of guilt, or if my mind tells me I may throw up my morning coffee. All day I do mental scans of my body, searching for signs of potential panic or sickness lurking just beneath the surface. But even when that scan comes back clean, I can easily be sideswiped by a full-blown panic attack. *What fun.*

That particular night, I worked hard to keep it at bay. Deep breaths, distractions, cold water, tapping. But this attack was taking off quickly. So, I told Reed, "I think I need to go for a walk. The cold air will help."

"Okay, let's go," he said, putting down his fork.

We clipped on Dex's leash and made our way down the rusty fire escape. The air was cold but there was no snow on the ground. Not yet. We walked laps around the University of Toronto campus and the small streets surrounding Reed's apartment while I took deep breaths and shook my hands repeatedly, trying to let the panic escape through my fingertips. But the nauseating pit of anxiety was growing fast, like a balloon being unrelentingly inflated in the deepest crevasse of my stomach.

I kept us pacing through dark, quiet streets for long enough that we were both shivering. I'd gone out without a jacket.

It had become clear this panic attack wasn't going to dissipate without more help and soon I'd have to call for backup. I also knew my dad was close by at my parents' condo by the day of the week.

So, through worried breaths and tapping hands, I told Reed, "I think I'm going to call my dad."

And that was all it took.

"Seriously? I've been outside freezing my ass off, for what?"

"I'm sorry but it's not getting better. I want to call my dad."

"Unbelievable."

He took off ahead of me, back toward his apartment. Perfectly attuned to even the slightest change in his movements, Reed's knees lifting just a little bit higher told me things may now turn ugly. I followed slowly behind, panic uprooting any sense of safety I'd ever had.

Reed skipped quickly up the fire escape, never glancing back. Dex and I followed — I needed my things. But when I got to his front door, it was locked. I knocked. And knocked. But no answer. Luckily, I had my cell phone, unluckily, I didn't have my coat and my dad was about to see me panicking alone, cold and locked out.

I sat myself on the curb and the frozen Toronto winter seeped through my jeans. A few minutes later, the screen door squeaked open at the top of the fire escape. Reed stepped onto the top stair, then threw a skateboard at me. It hit the sidewalk with a loud crash, the sound echoing down the empty street. Without flinching, Reed retreated into the warmth of his bedroom.

I stared at the skateboard, entirely unsurprised by his actions and yet, as always, shocked.

Mortified at the thought of my dad seeing me sitting pathetically on the sidewalk in the freezing cold without my boyfriend, I knew I had to write a story. I needed a reason as to why — in the world — I'd be left to face the toothy monster of anxiety on my own.

The familiar lights of my dad's car lit the sidewalk. Dex and I hopped in.

"Reed went upstairs to grab my bags but I don't need them. Let's just go. I'll text him," I lied.

I can't imagine he believed me, but he let it slide.

In the car, my dad spoke to me with endless patience and tried to calm me down. The juxtaposition in treatment was painful, turning my stomach even more, leaving me trapped and more alone than I ever knew was possible.

"What's wrong, Honey? Talk to me." His eyes were full of empathy and love. It always hurt him to see me drowning.

"I just can't calm down. I can't calm down. I don't know what's wrong, I'm scared I'm going to throw up. I can't breathe." My lungs were hungry for air, and I wanted burst through the windshield.

"You're okay, Honey. Take a breath. Relax. We're okay. What can I do to help you right now?"

In my dad's car, there is always sixties or seventies music playing and the seats invariably smell like untouched leather. I scanned my surroundings to bring myself into my body, back into reality. His Tim Hortons coffee cup was still in the cup holder from the drive in that morning, every crevasse of leather in the car perfectly clean, his pristine phone charging with a cord still mostly coiled with a white twist-tie. These details were the smallest tastes of my real life. My alternate universe where I was anchored and, above all else, safe.

Gentleness was becoming a distant memory, and so was being met with kindness without the threat of a fiery detonation. I knew I was really starting to lose myself when I flinched in anticipation of my dad hitting the steering wheel in anger and frustration toward me. Nothing — nothing — could be further from who my father was and is. He's calm, kind, and steady. The kind of dad who sat us down and explained why he said no instead of feeding us the tried-and-true "because I said so." The kind of dad who always answered our calls even when he was in a meeting. The kind of dad who was thrilled if we showed up unannounced at his office. The kind of dad who let us cover him in hair clips and Beanie Babies.

Subconsciously bracing myself for anger from my safest place, my father, was a wake-up call; my perception of men was rapidly changing.

At the condo, my dad turned on the TV to try to pull my focus. He ate dinner and talked to me as I circled, gasping for air and rhythmically tapping my chest. The panic attack wasn't subsiding as I hoped it would once I was with my dad; it was actually snowballing and the walls were beginning to cave in. I thought my dad probably hadn't bought the Reed story. I knew Reed was angry, and I knew I might be punished for choosing to leave him for my father. He had just locked me out and whipped a skateboard at me. Plus, that rich butter chicken was now sitting high in my stomach. I pictured orange mush coming back up and landing all over the floor of the condo, the sound it would make hitting the dark wood floors. I pictured us having to clean it up. Panic crashed into my body, and I took a deep, frantic breath, trying to push it back down.

My parents have always been home free when I'm having an anxiety attack. The fact that it wasn't subsiding once I was safely with my dad was scaring me. If this didn't help, I wasn't sure what would. A wave of intense helplessness seeped into my mind.

Drained and weak from hours of panic, I climbed into my dad's bed and somehow managed to fall asleep but only for a few short minutes before jolting awake. I sat up pulsing with panic and began dry heaving over the bed. Sure that I was about to vomit, I bent over so I wouldn't vomit on myself. I started crying, screaming, and grabbing for my father, yelling that I wanted to die. Then I fell back asleep. A few minutes later, I woke up and began dry heaving once again.

My dad sat next to me on the bed trying to centre my focus and settle me down. He occasionally reached out to put his hand on my shoulder, but I jumped backwards, out of reach. Anyone or anything touching me felt like hands around my throat. I couldn't breathe. So, he stepped away to give me some space, only for me to desperately scream, "Don't leave me! Please. Stay with me, Dad, please!" I was out of control. "I would rather die right now than feel this way. I want to die. You have to help me. Please. I want to die."

I meant it.

My dad looked back at me with soft, worried, eyes. "I wish I could take this all away from you."

I didn't see a way out.

It was a night from hell. The walls threatened me, inching closer, pushing away the air. Moments of sleep were peppered by terrified fever dreams and repeating song lyrics. I dripped with sweat and tried to think of the relief of death. Everything was wrong and bad and I wondered if I wanted to live. My anxious mind pined for death, and it didn't scare me but instead, brought me comfort and momentary calm. If dying was the only way to stop the reality of this moment and beyond, that was okay.

But eventually, I tired myself out like a child after a tantrum. My dad made up the pull-out couch and I fell into a deep sleep.

He's either the best thing that ever happened to me, or my very worst nightmare.

CHAPTER 14

I slept through my dad leaving for work. Body aching with a fear hangover, I skipped class and spent the day with Dex trying to recover in the safety of the condo. Something about it made me feel untouchable. It was an escape from my real life, from the toxicity, the belittling, the manipulation, the abuse, the lying. At the condo, I could pretend I was home with my parents, like I never moved out, never met Reed, was never thrown against the wall. Momentarily, I was out of reach of my worsening reality and able to visit the little place in my mind that still remembered how it felt to be a child, before my leaves began to wilt.

From somewhere under the mess of blankets, my phone was vibrating. I threw the comforter, frantically searching and hoping to see Reed's name, knowing it was extremely unlikely.

But much to my surprise, this time, it was him.

"Hello?" I sat up.

"Hey, how's it going?" Reed's casual voice appeared, and my body turned rigid and angry.

I paused, unable to grasp how he could ask me something so blatantly normal.

"I mean . . . Not great." I took a moment and considered my words carefully. Confronting him about what he'd done would do nothing but push him away. He would deny, downplay, make me feel as though I'd made it up, that he was the one wronged. I considered what I would get from him, and if it was worth it. Finally, I said, "I had a bad panic attack last night. I was almost vomiting. It was awful."

"That sucks. Are you feeling any better now?"

I stared blankly forward, expressionless and numb, listening to the hum of the city, stories above Bloor Street. Did he really believe he hadn't done anything to contribute to my state of mind the night before? Did I overreact? Did I expect too much? How could he possibly not acknowledge what he did? How was I living in this alternate universe free of accountability and facts?

Instead, I said, "Feeling a bit better. I'm going to stay here for a while, though. I'm exhausted and I need to rest." My eyes filled with tears. The loneliness was unbearable.

That sliver of him was a relief. A crumb more than silence registered as a teaspoon of support. Every other time he'd hurt me or I'd done something to upset him, Reed would take the opportunity to punish me further and disappear, only to reappear once he felt I had served my penance for my sins. Consistently having the rug pulled out from under me — only to be told that I had tripped — wreaked havoc on my ability to trust my foundation and judgment. It made me feel like I had nowhere left to fall back on but the familiarity of that uncertainty; it became my only perceived stability. As I slowly lost my mind wondering what I had done wrong, he would casually resurface. I realize now that this conditioned me to crave his presence and hold onto him even tighter, however I could.

Reed calling me, unprompted, was as grand a gesture as came from him. Why he reached out instead of vanishing, I didn't know. Maybe he knew I was with my family, and if they were around to hear this phone call, it was good optics. Maybe he was worried they were telling me to leave him, and he was attempting to lure me back in with a shred of thoughtfulness. Usually, his mind games worked.

Sitting amongst my old life, my real life, it became even clearer that the gap was widening between Reed and the softness of my other world.

Empty and defeated, I lay in bed all day, knees pulled to my chest, focused on regaining my strength and recovering from the immediate trauma. *What if it happens again today? What if I start dry heaving and now I'm alone?* My mind told me I wouldn't be able to cope. So, I stayed under the covers until the sun went down, surrounded by my dad's things. Soon, the glow of the city poured into the condo, and the CN Tower peeked out from between two neighbouring buildings. My mind and body still felt disconnected and somehow fake, as if I was outside of my physical shell, watching.

Reluctantly, I rolled up the comforter, threw my sheets in the washing machine, and folded the pull-out couch back into a living room.

Leaving behind a pitch-black apartment, I locked the door and made my way to the subway, Dex following at my feet. As I waited on the Bay Street platform, the bags under my eyes pulling toward the tiled ground, I opened my phone and texted Blake. *Hey! What are you doing? Wanna grab a drink?* A few minutes later she replied, *Ya come up! I'm in your building.*

Dexter on my lap, each stop brought me closer to home, and I filled with dread. I dropped Dex off in my own unit and checked myself in the mirror; tired, but passable, and I didn't want to be alone with my thoughts any longer.

Upstairs, I knocked on Logan's door. Blake answered.

"Hey!" Blake paused. "Hey . . ." Her piercing blue eyes looked into mine, full of concern.

"What?" I asked, with faux confusion and a forced smile.

"What's going on?" She asked as I followed her into the living room.

"Just . . . Uh . . . Just a bad night, I guess," I told her. She looked beautiful, as she always did, and free. I filled with envy. "My anxiety is just really bad."

Blake's eyebrows furrowed. She looked at me sharply, seeing right through it all. "This isn't normal. You know that, right?"

"I know." Without any defence, I looked down at my feet.

Whether Blake was talking about my mental health or Reed, I didn't know. Either way, she was right.

I'm drowning. You're holding my head under water. You're controlling me. Get off. I'm not strong enough for you.

CHAPTER 15

Reed was still working at a nearby camera store to help pay his bills, not yet able to be a full-time photographer. Most days, he spent his shifts emailing me articles about how compatible our signs were or pictures of Kurt Cobain in a dress.

Occasionally, during an afternoon shift, I wandered over to deliver snacks or keep him company. And on one particular day, although the other side of the glass was bustling with busy pedestrians, inside, it was quiet. That's when one of us suggested we sneak into the washroom. I'd never done anything like it, but with Reed, there were always new ideas.

He went first and I followed, locking the door behind me.

But it wasn't long after we started having sex that Reed put an end to it and began to collect himself. This was surprising. Yes, we were in a bathroom and yes, he was on the clock, but I was skeptical any of this would have stopped him.

Sex was what drove Reed. I believe it was his very favourite drug, the thing he most thirsted for. He was unassuming about his addiction; you wouldn't find him approaching the most beautiful women, pushing his hair back and handing out cheeky compliments. Instead, he'd sit in the corner, hands folded gently on his lap, occasionally looking up with only his eyes. He focused his attention with quiet, thoughtful precision. He'd wait for you to approach, and once you were in his orbit, he got you into his bed and became a different animal. No longer quiet and unrestrained, he was confident. Eventually, it was abundantly clear to me: He loved sex with a consuming ferocity I previously didn't know was possible.

Confused, I watched Reed through the bathroom mirror. Unsure if I even wanted the answer, I asked anyway, "That's it?" He let out a quick *mhm* before unlocking the bathroom door and disappearing back into the store. Reed didn't like having to explain himself. He never made it easy and rarely felt I deserved any explanation, but I didn't understand.

Back in our neighbouring swivelling office chairs, I contemplated my next move. Something inside of me felt rejected, like he'd been bored or uninterested enough to leave. Just as I opened my mouth to hesitantly, gently, ask for some answers, Reed reached into his backpack, pulled out his wallet and handed me two twenty-dollar bills.

"What's this for?"

"A Plan B," he said.

"What? You . . . ?" I took a second to catch up.

"Well, you didn't think I just stopped, did you?" he asked.

He was right, I knew him better than that.

A wave of defeat washed over me.

This is a complicated one for me to unravel. Admittedly, there were times earlier in our relationship when we'd mutually consented to this very thing. Back when we were happier, me weaker. But this time, we hadn't. I hadn't. Knowing the past had left me unsure whether it was fair to be upset. I wasn't even sure it was wrong. I wondered: In this very particular situation, did consenting once mean consenting in perpetuity? Could I blame him for thinking I'd be okay with it this time, too? I had trouble accepting that something fun had taken an odd and sad turn, leaving me questioning myself, questioning him, questioning my safety, and questioning whether I was being respected at all. That, mixed with a sprinkle of desperate denial and an ache to be all the things he wanted.

I'm hard-pressed to believe he didn't detect the sadness washing over my face. But he didn't mention it.

Consent. It's something I thought I understood until this relationship and its sometimes sneaky nuance. Looking back, I had questionable experiences before Reed. Most (if not, all) women have. Like the time a good friend walked me back to my hotel after I'd had a couple drinks only to kiss me right as I fell asleep. That night I was drunk, we were with a large group of friends, including my older sister, and nothing set off the alarm bells we women have. In no way did I feel the need to have my guard up — not with him. This friend walked me home, presenting himself as the thoughtful, protective knight in shining armour He knelt beside the couch, tucked me in, then slowly leaned in and kissed me on the lips just as my eyes drifted shut. Even through my drunken haze and foggy mind, as his mouth inched closer to mine, I believed two things: First, he wasn't drunk, and second, it wouldn't be happening if I was sober. He knew had I been sober, I wouldn't have allowed it. But he had me alone and vulnerable as my sister and our friends slept in nearby bedrooms.

When I woke up the next morning, having clearly remembered what he'd done, I never thought of it as an issue of consent. I saw it as nothing more than bizarre behaviour from a relatively close friend of mine. I wondered if our sometimes flirty relationship made it okay. Marley and I shared a collective, *Ew, what?*, but I didn't think much of it beyond that. I didn't see how indisputably disgusting his behaviour was. This was over a decade ago and consent wasn't as much at the forefront of the conversation back then.

As an adult, I see it as a trusted friend seizing my vulnerability as his own opportunity.

Another time, I was at the gastroenterologist searching for answers to my relentless IBS symptoms which, at the time, were controlling my life. The doctor was in a strange North Toronto building with mostly empty, dark offices. After a pretty humiliating appointment, I leaned against the exam table, bum still sticking out, beginning to get dressed. This quite old male doctor continued to talk to me about my symptoms, and as he walked behind me back to his desk, he placed his hand gently onto my lower back and slid it down quickly to graze my bum. The moment was quick and bizarre. It wasn't a grab, but instead, casual and familiar, as if he was my boyfriend sneaking behind me to grab a glass.

I wasn't scared or threatened, but I did immediately clock how inappropriate and gross it was, especially given that he had just had me in a very vulnerable position. I believed I was safe, even though he was a man and it was awkward, because he was a doctor doing his job. Suddenly, that didn't feel true.

But I wasn't going to make it into a big deal, so instead of questioning his behaviour, I questioned my interpretation.

Desperate for help and having waited months to see a specialist, I believe I still saw him for a second appointment.

Those two seconds have always stuck with me.

Women are at the mercy of men in so many ways, big and small.

I described the threat of men to a man in my life like this: Imagine every time someone comes into your house — a plumber, an electrician — it is instead a Rottweiler. You don't know if this Rottweiler is friendly — it may very well be — but just as easily, it could be aggressive and dangerous. Now you are potentially in danger in your own home, alone, cornered and vulnerable. You try to make yourself smaller and keep it happy, but not too happy that it gets comfortable and ends up close enough to bite.

I once asked another man in my life, "Can you imagine — really, truly imagine — what it would feel like to walk around worried you could be raped anywhere you go? Can you imagine what it feels like to be alone in an elevator with someone twice your size who could sexually assault you? Can you wrap your head around the fact that women exist every day knowing we could be raped by someone we know?"

He paused and really thought about it before saying, "No. I can't even imagine."

In 2024, an interesting question swept TikTok. The question asked women: Would you rather be alone in the woods with a man or a bear? Overwhelmingly, women chose the bear. This isn't surprising. According to a 2024 World Animal Foundation report, globally there are approximately forty bear attacks annually, and your chance of being attacked by a bear is one in 2.1 million. Compare that statistic to a UN Women's website that states: "Globally, eighty-five thousand women and girls were killed intentionally in 2023. Sixty per cent of these homicides — 51,100 — were committed by an intimate partner or a family member. The data shows that 140 women and girls die every day at the hands of their partner or a close relative, which means one woman or girl is killed every ten minutes."

According to Womankind Worldwide, "the most dangerous place for a woman is the home."

Being a woman vulnerable to the whims of men is unrelenting, and the older I get, the more terrified I become. An alarming number of men seem to be fuelled by deep, poisonous aggression and a desire for dominance, lest they feel smaller, even for a moment. That desire to be dominant is so intriguing to me. It's as if they know how scary it is to be vulnerable, to be physically weaker and at risk, yet instead of working to dismantle the exact systems they're clearly so afraid of, and the women in their lives experience daily, a large group of men make it their driving mission to uphold their fragile idea of power.

To me, this reeks of fear.

Fear of rejection, fear of humiliation, fear of appearing weak.

On Instagram, there is an account (which I refuse to name) with over 95K followers, whose bio reads: *Men hitting back — when the tables turn!*

Deep breathing my way through it, I scrolled.

One video (with 39.8K likes and 1.4M views as of this writing) showed a young woman — maybe in high school — hitting a boy her age. She swings at his stomach six times as he tries to turn away. The boy then tucks his phone into his pocket, brings his fist back, and violently punches the girl in the face and side of the head five times (from what we can see before they disappear out of frame). Written at the top of the video are the words: *This page only posts* WOMEN *getting* EQUALITY . . .

Some comments on the video include:

That's how you become a man

Real boys never beat women. Real [men do].

NOOOOOO DON'T HIT [women] LIKE THAT *u must do it harder than that*

Not satisfied enough she should be on the floor with blood covering her face

Equal rights and lefts

According to the dumpster fire that is that comment section, the boy was only trying to "protect himself," a grace often not afforded to women. But, if I may paint with broad strokes for a quick moment, physical strength is a place where most men and women can never truly be equal. Violence will also never be "equal" when tens of thousands of women are killed by their intimate partners or family members globally each year. Instagram pages such as these (which also show non-violent "Karens" being punched in the face or thrown to the ground in parking lot arguments, for example), are nothing more than a place for men to commiserate about their hatred of women.

It's incredibly revealing that this is how they choose to spin the big scary word: *equality*.

A 2023 Statistics Canada report noted the following: "By gender, the highest rate of police-reported intimate partner violence in 2023 was among women and girls aged twelve to twenty-four years (752 per 100,000 population), a rate nearly seven times higher than that for men and boys of that age group (111 per 100,000 population). Among all adults aged twenty-five to sixty-four years, the rate was more than three times higher for women (688 per 100,000 population) than for men (210 per 100,000 population)."

Note the word "reported."

Evan Rachel Wood — actor, activist, and survivor of domestic violence — shared the following via social media: "There is no consent in a domestic violence relationship. Period. Once the threat of violence is there, you comply. You don't consent."

The presence of violence changed absolutely everything for me. But where I felt that shift the most was when it came to sex. Once Reed's body had been used against me, after I'd been thrown against the wall and slapped across the face, the possibility of true consent was lost, as was any sense of safety when it came to sex.

The incident with Reed in the bathroom is one I take much more seriously now than I did at the time. I'd agreed to take a Plan B pill in the past. Because of that, I wasn't sure how to make sense of it. It didn't feel any of the ways I expected an issue of consent to feel. Unlike the friend and gastroenterologist, Reed's body was familiar, he was my boyfriend, and I thought, most importantly, I'd said yes to it before. But he knew I wasn't on birth control and we weren't using any form of birth control that day. He also knew the other times we decided to do this we'd talked about it, we'd agreed. He must have known I required a conversation. Why did he think this time would be any different?

I associated lack of consent or coercion with a feeling of fear, pressure, and violence. This situation didn't necessarily check those boxes, but it did feel wrong. I felt taken advantage of, being kept in the dark about what was being done to my own body. I felt the choice had been made for me. If, at the end of the day, I had gotten pregnant, it was going to happen to my body. It was going to change my life. It would be my psychological and physical burden to carry. Not his. There was no excuse for not consulting me this time, just as we had discussed it before. And on top of all of that, I wasn't being met with any kindness, thoughtfulness, or gentleness about it. My hurt feelings were plastered across my face as I felt just a little bit lonelier, just a little bit dirtier. He'd used me just the way he wanted then had me handle the repercussions, volunteering the bare minimum of explanation and attention. He expected me to disappear and clean up his mess. I thought maybe I hadn't made it clear, and maybe I had a role to play in blurring the lines. A simple, "I'm sorry, I should have asked this time, too. We usually talk about it first. Are you okay?" could have changed everything. That didn't seem to be a language he'd ever learned.

But also, maybe if abuse hadn't been present between us, consent could have been a different conversation, one where we were on even ground. Maybe if he hadn't done numerous other things to my body without consulting me, I wouldn't have seen it the same way. Maybe if he hadn't shoved me. Maybe if he hadn't travelled with that black plastic bag without ever truly consulting me on its contents. Maybe if he'd stopped slapping me across the face when I asked him to. Maybe if he asked me once how I felt about what we were doing, or if I was okay with it. Maybe if he stopped when I was visibly upset or when I blatantly asked him to. Maybe if he'd ever made it clear that my feelings were the priority. Maybe if he stopped suggesting we do the things I'd already said no to. Maybe then I would have seen this situation differently. But he didn't. So I don't.

If we were healthy enough for communication, real, thoughtful communication, I could have spoken up and said, "Why didn't you ask me this time?" He could have apologized, heard me, seen me, listened to me. Through talking, the threat could have evaporated from these experiences, but Reed was driven by power and dominance. In his eyes, we would never be equal.

To me, this reeks of fear. Fear of losing control of me, fear of losing.

The version of assault we're exposed to in movies or the horrific stories which reach the top headlines in the news unknowingly become the bar with which we measure the confusing experiences we may unfortunately end up having in our own lives. The most indisputable forms of assault are the stories we tuck away in our back pockets as the framework for what these things look like. So, when we hear a word like rape it conjures up very specific imagery: maybe a scene in a movie or a vicious case covered in the latest Netflix docuseries. If those stories represent one end of the spectrum, there is a vast murky area behind it. It's an area populated by stories that don't make the news, complete with landmines of intimate partner violence, grooming, violent sex, victim-blaming, attempts at leaving, and self-doubt.

With the world partially desensitized to even the most horrific of abuse stories, acknowledging moments that aren't as shocking to the ear can feel like screaming into space. These experiences don't fit into dramatic snapshots of irruptive violence or photo evidence of a black eye. To be clear, my intention would never be to compare these two valid and damaging realities, but rather to shed light on the perceived grey areas which gleefully cultivate shame and uncertainty.

This uncertainty plagued my sexual relationship with Reed. I constantly felt out of my depth. But it seemed to me that Reed had found exactly what he was looking for in my blatant inexperience. He liked that I was "new." I was a blank slate — wide-eyed, young, and fresh — and he was eager to further get his hands on me. He set out to corrupt my young brain (something he told me frequently). And that's exactly what he did.

I became an active participant.

Reed took his time and kept himself bridled in our early days. He lowered me slowly into his world, careful not to make any sudden movements which might scare me away. In the beginning he guided and taught me, mostly without words — just gentle, teaching nudges. He introduced me to the things he wanted me to know, taught me about my own body, and over time, without any real frame of reference, I found myself in a rich, fulfilling sexual relationship. I hadn't known such an exciting underground world existed. We had this thing to do when we were bored, when we were having a good day, when we were having a bad day. When we were angry. When we made up. When I wanted him all to myself.

Reed's infatuation with my body was like being under a white-hot spotlight. He liked to examine every inch, often consumed entirely in his own world, seemingly unaware that I was still present inside of that skin. The fixation didn't revolve around a desire to please me or even himself, but rather, from an angle of sheer appreciation. He loved it. Every part of it. Occasionally, his fascination and nothing-is-off-limits approach would make me shy, and I instinctively shrank away from his intensity and non-existent embarrassment. But he quickly chased any fears away, showering me with genuine assurance that my body was perfect and he would never tire of me. I believed him. I still believe him. He practically worshipped my body, which bolstered my confidence and unearthed my own desire to explore with him. He made it feel okay. Nothing could break his focus or tear him away as he gave himself to me entirely. I loved how he looked at me, as if I were a present for opening.

At one point, sex with Reed was one of the best parts of my life. But, quite clearly, it didn't stay that way.

Experiences that at one time we shared started to feel forced. I began to be pushed a little too far, where it hurt or he held on a little too long so it became hard to breathe. They were moments I had trouble labelling; I didn't know what was normal. You don't know what you don't know. There were times that felt wrong, when his desire to be aggressive reared its head more than I think even he intended. But the moments that confused me most were when Reed was happiest. My young brain couldn't make sense of it — it was too complex for a young mind that was only just learning the most basic rules of a sexual relationship.

In an effort to mentally tidy up, I decided that, when in a relationship with an adult man, there must be things one partner does strictly for the other's enjoyment, certain things you grin and bear. It took dating other people to finally see that this is not true or normal. Reed was simply pushing me too far without ever prioritizing my comfort. He thirsted for the very things I didn't want to do — and I knew that. He seemed to get off on having his way with my body knowing I previously objected. It didn't matter if my words and face were opposed, he could continue to enjoy it, seemingly without a grain of hesitation. I know his strong hands could feel me pulling back, muscles tensing, instinctively wanting to push his body away as I fought my own body's wishes.

Eventually, saying no to sex didn't feel like an option. Not really. If I didn't want to, he found another way to use my body and still get what he wanted. If I drew the line at hitting me across the face, as I had, he just wouldn't use his hands. Reed would persuade me until I caved or do it anyway and expect forgiveness. If all else failed, he would put in the time and simply convince me, flatter me, tell me how badly he wanted it. And I would yield, unable to resist the delight of being the one to deliver.

It's a strange thing when these very singular experiences happen during a first brush with real sexuality; where do you go from there? An element of danger accompanied Reed and sex. He showed me one way sex could be, and it was never dull. He was a rare breed, complicated, dark, guarded, yet wildly open. I was exposed to him before I had my own ideas, preferences, or any real form of comparison. Add abuse and my experiences began to jumble. How do you make sense of this thing, this brand-new part of your life making you feel on top of the world, and at the very same time, the smallest speck of dust?

Reed and I spent most of our time together at our apartments. It was spring, and he'd said goodbye to the blue bedroom and moved into a studio apartment a few blocks north. The same bed lay on the ground in the corner. Eventually, he built four posts and hung a sheet after too many fights about Reed reading into the night when I had early class the next morning. His insomniac routines didn't welcome interruption, especially in that studio apartment.

Most days, Reed could be found working cross-legged on the floor, the thick hair that made my knees weak sticking out of his black hoodie. There was usually psychedelic music playing, adding to the eeriness already lingering. This apartment was a still collection of quirky, twisted knick-knacks. Books and prints lay all over the floor, turtles swam around a small tank à la Cobain, small tins of weed on the table. The bathroom tiles were cracked and the bathtub was sprinkled with limescale. Any place Reed inhabited morphed into an artist's lair.

At first glance, Reed seemed to prioritize his body and mind, at least, this was the case in the early hours of the morning. Come evening, he sunk into self-destruction with drinks and drugs, his true self pouring from each pore. Reed believed he would die before twenty-seven and often hinted at taking it into his own hands, occasionally even threatening to kill himself by stepping off the curb as we walked a busy sidewalk.

"I wouldn't kill myself in front of you," he told me with a smirk. "It would mess you up forever."

I looked up and met his green eyes. "I can't tell if that's a joke or not."

"Ah, I'll never tell."

Reed was drawn to a very specific corner of the world, one which acknowledged so much darkness. His interests were never mainstream or superficial. He read about Buddhism and watched movies with subtitles that only played at small indie theatres around town. That isn't me, and it never was. This brought on many arguments about me and my interests "distracting" him from his projects. He felt I took him away from the things he was trying to accomplish (though I was never quite sure what those things were). This fight usually led to Reed listing my interests as being "shopping and watching movies," or other *less important* things. His digs were intended to make me feel like a paddling pool while he was an ocean. So, when I arrived one day to find he'd downloaded *Keeping Up with the Kardashians* for me, I saw it as quite the gesture. Reed would never watch reality television. But it was a compromise; I had something to do, so he could work without "distraction."

I was lying flat on my stomach as the Kardashians played from the foot of the bed, and a little while into the show, Reed put down his book and made his way over to me. I felt him climb onto the bed and begin to make it abundantly clear — in all those little established ways every couple has — he wanted to have sex.

"I don't really feel like it," I told him.

For a few seconds he continued to try, and I continued not to take the bait.

"I really don't feel like it," I told him as I kept my eyes glued to the laptop.

Then I heard the unsettling words from behind me, "Just watch the show."

My muscles tensed.

My boyfriend slid my pants halfway down my legs, lifted my shirt partway up my back, and climbed on top of me from behind as *Keeping Up with the Kardashians* continued to play. I did my best to mentally check out, as instructed. The sounds of a show which usually brought me comfort and entertainment in my most monotonous hours now became the soundtrack to something else. The mundane thrashing against the backdrop of complex violation chilled my insides.

I looked back, trying to make sense of the moment as it was unfolding on top of me. Maybe he'd see the look on my face and realize. Maybe he'd see that he'd misinterpreted the moment. But neither happened. So maybe it was me who'd misunderstood. I thought about simply giving in, flipping over, and participating. Removing my own pants or shirt fully could reframe the situation, small actions that would transform it from something violating to mutual, as we'd done countless times before. But my body said no. He'd climbed on top of me and was now inside of me, and I was not participating.

A moment beyond saving.

I didn't yell at him to get off. I didn't fight. I lay like a doll while my boyfriend who I'd had sex with countless times before had sex with my body. It felt wrong, but only to a certain point. With equal truth to my paralyzed mind, I knew no part of what was physically happening to me was new. I didn't feel taken advantage of. Or maybe I did. I wasn't scared. Or maybe I was. *Maybe he doesn't know I'm not participating. Should this feel wrong or is it okay? Am I being difficult, as his tone is alluding? Maybe nothing is even wrong.*

But he was someone who'd been violent, and as Evan Rachel Wood said, once there's been violence, we don't consent, we comply. He was someone I loved irreplaceably but was also scared of, someone I didn't trust to prioritize respect. I was in too deep to see it clearly for myself. *Do these things happen in adult relationships? Is this why sitcoms joke about men always wanting to have sex? Maybe this happens when people have been sleeping together for a while. Maybe it isn't that serious. We have sex all the time.*

But things were different when *no* no longer seemed to be an option.

I kept my eyes focused forward and did what I could to understand.

The clearest thought in my mind was that he was ruining it. I wanted to scream that he kept ruining us. We worked so hard to get to where we were. We'd been through so much already from sleeping together casually, to a few months apart, to now being a couple. He was all I wanted, and we'd finally sorted ourselves out. He was taking it all away.

At the time, that was the worst part.

Once he climbed off the bed, I sensed a shift within myself. I knew how it looked from the outside — one body participating and one not. I felt he wanted me on his terms, whenever he saw fit, however he saw fit, without the desire to understand how it made me feel and without the desire to understand what I wanted.

As much as I tried to convince myself otherwise, I knew on some level what happened wasn't right but decided not to pay it too much attention.

It was around this time that I often fantasized someone would tell Aidan I'd gone from the safety of our small town, the safety of his hockey games and basement couch, to being thrown against the wall by my throat and lying still like a doll. I dreamt of my phone lighting up with his name and the promise to come get me.

Something inside of me changed after my sexual relationship with Reed. The lightness vanished, the fun was taken away, and it's never really come back. He opened my eyes to everything, showed me too much, then left me to make sense of it alone. The wrongness between Reed and me became the very thing that made it feel special. I began seeking more of that same darkness wherever I could find it, eventually asking him to pour more of his salt in my wounds. Maybe it was my belief that I needed to nurture our darkness in order to keep us alive. Our roots were rotten.

Sexual experiences between us which should have been gentle and safe were instead veiled in threat, complete with cold shoulders of neglect and punishment. There were countless times that felt wrong in my bones. Many moments where I felt a particular sadness radiating from my brain down to the tips of my toes. Times I wished I'd been carefully, lovingly considered but wasn't. I think back on them now and wish I'd spoken up or tried a little bit harder to protect myself, but those shades of grey had me filled to the brim with self-doubt.

I can feel my layered feelings about sex creep in during a sex scene in a movie. I feel a lurch in my stomach, overtaken by sudden guilt, nausea, and sweaty palms. I'm not sure if it's fear for the woman on screen or if it simply triggers my most stressful, shameful memories with Reed. Part of me believes if he knew he'd taken this specific piece of me away, he'd be proud. I'm not sure that part of my life will ever fully move on without him; he's a part of my makeup, drew me the map of my body — and it doesn't feel good.

I came across a joint Instagram post from @teachusconsent and @feminist addressing the definition of sexual assault. The caption read, *Was it a "bad sexual experience" or was it sexual assault.* This was immediately intriguing to me, as it's a question I've spent years trying to answer.

Part of the post read:

> *Sexual assault covers many different types of sex crimes.*
>
> *Many people don't know what counts as sexual assault. Many victim-survivors don't realize they've been assaulted and just call it a "bad experience," "uncomfortable sex," or "pressured sex." For many, learning about true consent is when they first come to terms with what they were subjected to. Many perpetrators don't understand that their actions are harmful and criminal, so they don't change their behavior.*

The post then goes on to list a few examples of what constitutes sexual assault, such as: forcing a partner into sexual acts they didn't agree to (consent must be specific to each act), forced oral sex, touching someone when they're asleep, and watching or filming someone without their consent.

The post was a tough read, but an important one. I wasn't looking out for these forms of sexual assault at eighteen, nineteen, twenty and was only just beginning to understand the intricacies and unspoken rules of sexual relationships. Especially when I'd found myself someone as wildly open, adventurous, and experienced as Reed, who I trusted to teach me. But as @teachusconsent also wrote, *Yes only counts if no can be (safely) said.*

I now believe that Reed sexually assaulted me countless times. It took distance and experience to admit it.

His carelessness with my body poisoned me on a cellular level. Years later, I would lie in bed next to new boyfriends and cry. I couldn't understand why I suddenly felt used, gross, and sad, even when I'd been gently considered. I wondered if most people roll over to wipe away tears and sniffle quietly.

Even when no lines were crossed, my past screamed for attention.

Something very strange is happening inside of me. Something is evolving and changing. Maybe I'm finally seeing things clearly.

CHAPTER 16

Thanks to the combination of my lack of trust in Reed and frequently being left alone in his apartment, I sometimes, admittedly, went looking for trouble. His notebooks lay around the floor, some hidden under trinkets on his dresser.

One day, I gave in.

Standing up from the mattress in the corner, I tiptoed through Reed's apartment to a notebook on the floor next to a pile of secondhand books. Sitting down in his usual spot, I held the notebook in my hands, trying to decide. One voice inside my head told me not to do it because it was an invasion of privacy. I'd be just as guilty as Reed when he looked through my phone. But then a little devil appeared on my shoulder. She told me it was time to take some control.

Careful not to leave any trace, I sat cross-legged and gently flipped through pages. Most of the scribbles I didn't understand — doodles, poems and pages of nonsense. Then I reached the end — the most recent pages — and written clear as day across the top were the words: *I don't want to be with her, but I don't want her to be with anyone else.*

The very thing I feared. He didn't want to be with me. It was my biggest nightmare spelled out in front of me, crystal clear, in my boyfriend's handwriting. I was too superficial, too boring, just a distraction. He was deep, creative, and intricate. I simply couldn't keep up.

Those specific words were especially chilling as it was one of two threats my mother warned my sisters and me about when we were kids. She used to tell us, "If a man hits you once, leave. Because if he hits you once, he will hit you again." The second was to beware of exactly what I'd just found. I thought of my mom's words, "There are men out there who would rather you be dead than see you with someone else. If they can't have you, no one can."

But I thought, no. That's dramatic.

I closed the notebook and gingerly placed it back onto the floor at exactly the same angle I'd found it.

Between reading those words and Reed getting home, I'd almost come around to the idea; if he didn't want to be with me, maybe this was my out. As much as it broke my heart, we were so convoluted, so broken, maybe this was the push I needed to gather my things and finally walk out the door. Maybe, just maybe, this was a blessing in disguise. Maybe he'd even *let* me leave.

My hurt feelings were smeared all over my face, and the second he laid eyes on me he asked what was wrong. After the inevitable back and forth every couple knows too well ("What's wrong?" "Nothing." "What's wrong????" "Nothing!"), I told him.

"Well, listen, I kind of did something bad. I read your notebook," I said, tail firmly between my legs.

"Okay . . . And?"

"I found something that just . . . made me really sad."

"Okay, what is it?" Dark eyes looked back at me, focused.

I didn't want to say it out loud.

"*I don't want to be with her, but I don't want her to be with anyone else.* Is . . . Is that true?" I tried my best not to cry.

With everything Reed had put me through, the fear, the disappearances, the degrading comments, the way he went through my phone — reading one of his journals was a drop in the bucket. Although I felt I'd stooped to his level, I couldn't find it in myself to feel too bad about it. Not after everything.

Instead of reacting with anger, as I suspected he would, he responded with a slightly gentler tone.

"I had a feeling you were going to go through my notebooks," he said.

"You did? Why?"

"I just knew because I left you alone here. So I wrote that there for you to see." He began unpacking his backpack.

I stood staring at him. "What do you mean?" I'd been left alone in his apartment many, many times before.

"I knew you'd go through it, so I wrote that there for you to see that I need time on my own. I need time to work on my projects, on my own." He spoke as if his message had been perfectly delivered.

"But . . . I don't get it. That's not what it says."

"I was just trying to show you that I need time on my own, and I knew you'd go looking through those." He repeated the words slowly, as if I should get it. "It was just a brief moment and a brief thought, anyway. I don't feel that way all the time, just sometimes we need to spend time apart."

I felt like I was losing my mind. Back then, I was unaware of gaslighting.

Reed's tone left room for an apology — from me — as if he was the one who was wronged. We stood across the apartment from each other, my brows furrowed and his eyes looking anywhere but back at mine. I knew these were complete lies, but I couldn't wrap my mind around his acrobatic bending of the truth to muster up a logical rebuttal. I felt a wave of fear ripple through me, but it wasn't the usual fear. Instead, it was panic at the stark realization that I was floating in a world free of reality.

Reed was willing to feed me anything his brain could conjure up if it meant winning. I wondered just how much I was willing to accept — how stupid I was willing to appear — in order to keep the peace. In order to keep him.

I felt the snap of one of our tethers break, and I detached myself from him just a little bit. He didn't want to be with me, but he didn't want me to be with anyone else. That is all it meant. Maybe I felt the same way about him.

Do I really think this is all I deserve?
No.

CHAPTER 17

Many months had passed since Reed and I filmed ourselves having sex. I didn't think about it often; there were many other shameful nights to keep me occupied. But that changed one day when I caught a glimpse of the video on Reed's laptop, and even though I hadn't seen it for some time, I noticed quickly that something was different. It took me a second to put my finger on it, but soon it clicked; Reed had cut himself out of the video entirely. He was nowhere. Not a trace.

I looked on in horror and a rush of heat inched from my feet to my neck.

"Wait, did you edit yourself out?" I felt sick.

"Well, why would I want to watch myself?" He said, as if stating the obvious.

My stomach leapt into the back of my throat and my fingers began to shake. In front of us was a compilation of me, alone, in my most vulnerable, intimate, personal moments. My entire foundation flashed before my eyes. This was a complete departure from what we originally agreed to do *together.* I'd been stripped of all reassurance. And now, in conjunction with everything else we'd experienced over the last ten months, it felt like an attack.

His words from that day in the blue bedroom replayed, *I'm in it too! Why would I want anyone to see it?*

Just like that, his promise to protect me floated weightless.

As I came back into my body and the world around me stopped spinning with quite as much force, I softened the fear in my eyes. Something inside me knew it was important that he not know the power this held.

From that moment on, the tape crept into my thoughts with every disappearance, angry glance, or degrading night in the weeks that followed, mentally torturing me with its existence. The parts I'd seen played on loop in my mind while he lay next to me, facing the wall. I was trapped, and I think we both knew it. Sex and fear were heated and fused months earlier, and I wondered if I would carry that anxiety with me forever.

Through thick, brutal embarrassment, I brought up the tape with my therapist. It was nearly impossible to say the words out loud, but I could physically feel the weight of it living in my chest, begging to come out. Somehow.

I looked at the floor and felt like throwing up.

"He has a video of us having sex. I feel like it's eating me alive. I can't escape the thoughts. I can't control them." I paused and took a breath. "Sometimes I wonder if the tape is the only reason I'm still with him, and if it didn't exist I would have already left. Maybe. I don't know."

It was my first time saying these words out loud, acknowledging the part of me that was beginning to imagine life after Reed.

My therapist leaned forward. "Are you worried about what he might do with it?"

"I guess so. I guess I don't trust him with it, and as unhappy as I am with him lately . . . I just feel like he has me in a position where . . . I don't know what he's capable of, so I feel like I'm stuck with him." I looked up at her. "Not that I *want* to break up with him, even."

"But these worries must be coming from somewhere. What do you think he's capable of?"

"Maybe the problem is that I really don't know."

I spoke my fears out loud, each word chosen carefully. If anyone heard directly from me that he was dangerous, there would be no turning back. I wasn't ready for anyone to hold me accountable for leaving. If friends knew, their helpful nudges reminding me I deserved better would feel like hands on my back pushing me out the front door. I wasn't ready. So instead, I walked a tightrope with my therapist, insinuating that I couldn't leave while never sharing exactly why that was. She suggested I delete the tape myself while he was out, and if he got angry once he realized, she said, "Who cares? It won't be your problem anymore." My heart sank. If Reed found out I deleted it, it would definitely be my problem. I was too exhausted and embarrassed to explain why it wasn't a plausible option.

Shortly after, I went up north for my sister's birthday.

Tucked away off a dirt road, my parents' log home was quiet and dark. With just the hum of the refrigerator and the occasional creaking of logs filling the silence, I sat cross-legged on their brown leather couch and stared forward. Everyone else was out, busy, living their lives. I sat alone, heavy from my reality, aching with shame.

I didn't know when it happened, or even how it happened, but somehow I'd ruined my life. Every page turned was the end. He'd stolen everything from me: faith in myself, connection to my family, excitement for adulthood. With the toss of my body, I was reformed.

My brain was full, thoughts buzzed violently, telling me there was no way out. Too many mistakes had been made, too much of myself given away.

I opened my parents' wine fridge and pulled out an unopened bottle of white wine. Alone at the kitchen island, I twisted off the cap and took a large, cold gulp. A light burn seeped down my throat into my empty stomach. Then I took another gulp. And another. Wandering around the house, bottle in hand, I searched for familiarity, reminders of my true self, but I couldn't find any. So, I took another gulp. And another.

Soon, my arms hummed and melted with a light heat, the bottle weighing less and less in my hand. I continued to walk around my parents' dark house, swimming through a fog of self-loathing.

White headlights flooded the entryway, pulling me away from my sadness and into my drunk body. Whoever it was would expect an explanation for my strange actions.

"Hello?" My sister's voice echoed from the breezeway.

"Hey," I said, rounding the corner, near empty bottle in hand. My sister was taking off her shoes, her boyfriend next to her doing the same.

She looked up at me. ". . . Hey. What are you doing?"

"Not much," I said, eyes glassy.

"Are you just drinking here alone?" My sister stared at me with deep concern and even deeper confusion.

"I mean . . . I've had a few glasses of wine. I was bored. Everyone is out," I justified.

"You okay?" Her boyfriend asked, turning on more lights to get a better look at me.

I focused on my sluggish tongue. "I'm fine."

The three of us settled at the dining room table, and I tried to mask any slurred words. They told me about their night. They'd been at her boyfriend's parents' house, and now they were going to watch a movie downstairs. My drunken haze watched the two of them with envy; my sister had no idea how lucky she was to be safe.

Eventually, I said goodnight and made my way up the stairs. I knew I was leaving them to talk about me, to worry, to feel in over their teenage heads. The old part of me cared, the new part of me didn't. At all.

I closed my bedroom door and reached down between the crevasse of my bed frame and mattress. There, I'd hidden a serrated steak knife. I lifted my left sleeve and began sawing at my inner arm, high enough that the cuts wouldn't be easily visible or damage the Abbey Road tattoo on my wrist. White wine pumped through my veins, dulling the pain.

The next morning, I woke up to a sting, my arm lined with pink cuts. Regret flooded over me in waves. The cold light of sobriety was humiliating.

Downstairs at the table, my sister sat with my parents.

"So, uh, what was—" She began to ask, as soon as I sat down. I whipped my head up and looked at my sister with desperate eyes, begging her to stop. Silently, she told me we'd have to talk about it eventually.

Back in the city, Reed pulled me into his chest and said, "Tell me you love me."

It was a small moment carrying big weight, evidence Reed must have been picking up on my slow detachment.

Throughout our relationship, I often told Reed, "Tell me you love me!"

With an eye roll and a little smile, he'd say, "I love you."

On this particular day, my eyes fell shamefully to the floor and I did my best to deflect. "I always tell you that."

I couldn't say the words. It felt wrong. I wasn't sure, but part of me was emotionally moving forward without him, beginning to pry myself from his grip. I wondered if I might only be around until he promised to delete the video, then I would walk out the door without looking back at his resentful eyes.

At the same time, I wasn't sure I'd ever be ready.

"Tell me you love me!" He said again, arms still wrapped gently around my shoulders, chin resting on the top of my head.

"I love you." This time, it was me whose words didn't match my eyes.

I loved him, and I knew I probably always would, but some part of me had shut off. Something inside of me had been pushed too far, made to feel too small, living in insecure, thin skin that didn't belong to me. He felt so different to me now, and love was the antithesis.

That night, after we turned out the lights, I stared at the ceiling. Reed's bed used to be the only place in the world I wanted to be. It used to make me happy when literally nothing else did. Reed had, in many ways, been the only thing that kept me alive. Now, we felt insincere and phony. I thought back a year earlier, sneaking down the block and knocking on Reed's door.

His voice suddenly appeared in the dark, "You're going to make some other guy so happy one day."

I froze. "Why would you say that?"

Reed rolled over to face me. "You know we can't be together."

Reed liked to push me away when he loved me most.

The next day, bolstered by the hope of relief and knowing we were slowly disintegrating, I brought up the tape.

I sat at the head of the bed, back against the wall. Reed was across the room on his laptop. My stomach flipped. "Hey, I have a question for you."

"What's up?" He turned to face me.

"I don't know why, but recently the tape we filmed has kind of been, like, bothering me. It's weighing on me. I don't know why. I just don't feel good about it lately." I paused for a moment of courage. "Can we delete it?"

Reed waited a moment before answering. "Why now?"

"I don't know, I just don't feel good about it, and I don't want to be bothered by something between us. I would feel much better if you just got rid of it for me. I'd feel . . . calmer or something." I did my best to sound unrehearsed. "Also, we said we'd watch it once then delete it, but that was months ago now."

Although inside I was begging, pleading, for him to release me, I steadied my outsides. If his attuned nose smelled a drop of desperation, he'd know he had me. I moved through his bedroom like a chess piece.

Flatly, he asked, "Is that the only reason you're here right now?"

His words pierced.

"Are you kidding?" I fired back.

But I couldn't believe just how easily he saw through me. I'd been clocking hours, working hard to keep up the facade — even going so far as to spend the night at his apartment, sleeping next to him, as my feelings faded and my nerves told me it wasn't safe.

"Do you really think that?" I sat up a little bit straighter.

"Maybe, yeah." Reed's reply was confident. "Am I right?"

With the exception of my therapist, no one in my life knew this tape was weighing heavily on me, so I knew for certain he hadn't been tipped off by going through my phone. The fact that he'd hit the nail square on the head threw me completely off-balance. I fumbled my way through a reassurance.

"That is definitely not the case. I would just feel better about us if it was gone, that's all. You have the real thing, anyway!"

I tried to smile while inside I calculated my next move. I began to feel suicidal thoughts bleeding through, spreading rapidly, like spilled ink. Then, the darkest thought of all: I wondered if I was trapped with him, alive, forever.

Acutely aware this was one of my only chances, I focused. I couldn't bring it up again. It was now or never.

So, I said, "I wouldn't be here all day and then sleep over just to get you to delete it." I wasn't even convincing myself. I felt terrible.

"Are you just going to leave me after I delete it?" He said vacantly.

I didn't have the answer to his question. But I looked into the eyes that I loved so much and said, "No. I'm not going to leave you."

I wasn't sure which was the truth. Every word of this conversation plunged me lower. Would I really leave him if he deleted it in front of me? Most of the time it felt like there would never be a reason big enough to walk away. How could I walk away knowing no one could ever be him? I was never going to be the same, could I face the new me alone? He'd burrowed deep under my skin, and sometimes I wasn't sure I even wanted him out. But for the first time, little whispers were telling me to run.

That day, he didn't delete it, and clearly I'd tried a little too hard to convince him when he started throwing his laptop into his backpack each time he left the apartment. He used to leave it so I could watch the shows he'd downloaded for me. But after that conversation he never left me and his computer unsupervised. I thought about grabbing the laptop and throwing it off the balcony while he was in the shower and dealing with the repercussions, as my therapist had sort of suggested (without the breaking part). I could throw it and run, as a desperate last attempt to free myself, a last attempt at reviving my past life, which was just days away from flatlining. I pictured the laptop smashing into little pieces all over the sidewalk. Then I pictured racing through the apartment to grab my things and leave before the hiss of the shower stopped. But the more I thought about it, the more I knew this would only light the very match I didn't want to light. I had no idea what I was up against. Destroying one copy wouldn't give me any peace of mind, but instead, bait him into proving he could not be controlled.

Then I thought of another time I was using his laptop.

I remembered flipping through files and my heart violently leaping into my throat after images of bare breasts took over the screen. I scanned the pictures for clues, wondering who it was, when it happened, where I thought he'd been that day. It took me a second. But then I realized. I was looking at images of my own naked body. Eventually, I pieced it together. They were from an intimate Skype call when I was in California and specifically had asked him not to take any screenshots. I wasn't sure which was worse, photos of myself I didn't know existed or photos of another woman that she'd sent to my boyfriend, when both had happened.

Stumbling across my own body, from the outside as a voyeur, I didn't recognize myself. It wasn't just *my* body anymore, and this somehow felt more violating than most other things he'd done to me. I trusted him. He was supposed to protect me and guard my body with equal fierceness. I still struggle to comprehend it. Something about his sneakiness, his deceitfulness, hurts my heart in a specific way. I was practically begging him to treat me well and not look at me like a piece of meat. He was supposed to keep my body safe.

I'm not sure when or why it finally happened, but the second time I tried, Reed was receptive. "Have you thought more about the tape?"

"Fine, if it means that much to you, we'll delete it. Okay?" His response was cold.

I stood over Reed's shoulder as he opened his laptop and dragged the file into the trash can.

"Now empty the trash," I instructed.

With the quiet sound of crumpling paper, the trash can emptied.

In that moment, I knew Reed most likely hadn't deleted every copy in his possession. That would have required a drastic change of heart (and a brand-new personality). It would have required his complete faith in how much I loved him and him being okay with laying down his sword. At my very centre I didn't feel any lighter, but I allowed myself to believe I'd finally seen what I needed to see. It was over. The war had ended and now I could focus on erasing him. I could start to move on and untangle myself from the complicated web of lies where he'd trapped me, start repairing my friendships, and wash my own blood from my hands. Maybe I would even start to hate myself less. Most importantly, without the tape hanging over my head, the bad memories would be mine alone to live with. My actions weren't going to affect anyone else in my life, and they weren't going to cause embarrassment beyond just myself. It was a memory I would carry around on my own back. I could do that. I could hate myself silently.

I played the game for a while longer, sleeping next to him, telling him I loved him, and lying — lying to him that my heart was still in the relationship and lying to myself that I was starting to let him go. In quiet moments, I thought back to the summer before. The intense heat of Reed's small bedroom, the crushing happiness, loving him so hard. I thought of what he used to represent: the guy I never thought would love me who wanted me bad. We galivanted around the city like high school crushes, unfailingly in love. And now, I was scared of him, searching for an exit, wondering how to get myself out alive. I wondered: Had he been hiding who he was last summer or was he just happy at the beginning? Did he change over the last year? Or was he simply pretending to be sweet and infatuated back then? Did he make sure I was in love before letting his true self show? Did he intentionally lay the groundwork only to be violent once I was in too deep to walk away? Or were we just more in love last year?

Over ten years later, I sat in bed reading Amia Srinivasan's *The Right to Sex*, specifically the essay titled "Talking to My Students About Porn." In it, she writes: "The camera in porn doesn't linger on the man's face, if it's shown at all; very often the camera is positioned so as to replicate his point of view. Where the male body is pictured, it is an active body, the agent of the film's action, the source of its motive desire and narrative progression. The only part of the male body to be given any real screen time is the erect penis — a stand-in for the viewer's own . . . Where is the woman viewer in all this?"

I'll admit, it was a revelation. I was late to the party, yes, but I finally got it; what was, in my eyes, a choice to do something together — the benefit being the act itself — was for him, something else. For Reed, the payoff was what came after. How naive of me. How naive am I, still, having only learned its true function years later?

My intention was never to become part of his collection, next to unwelcomed screenshots and videos of strangers. But that's what I became, trimmed and edited to fit his desires alone.

There is a framed photo of me just outside my bedroom at my parents' house. I look about ten, standing under an apple tree on our property. I remember the day it was taken. Tiny shoulders, big front teeth, long undamaged red hair, and freckled porcelain skin. For years that photo haunted me. Something about it perfectly encapsulated the childhood I felt I'd ruined with the existence of the tape. Each time I walked by that frame, my stomach would sink with guilt for wrecking her, for throwing away that girl who was free of regret and sexuality. I smudged her innocence. On days I didn't feel like inflicting torture, I avoided the eyes of that girl and her big front teeth. Other days, when I wanted to dig that freshly sharpened knife in deep, I forced myself to look at her and face the person I vandalized.

LEAVING

I will not walk away. I will run away.
Run, Callie.

CHAPTER 18

My uncle Mike, who had big, sleepy eyes and a sharp sense of humour, was born with cystic fibrosis, a rare inherited progressive disease that causes mucus to build up in the body, making it difficult to breathe. When Mike was a newborn, my grandparents were told he likely wouldn't live beyond a few months. When he beat those odds, doctors warned he likely wouldn't live past three, then seven, then ten.

Mike lived to thirty-seven. He had good periods, allowing him to build a successful career in advertising as a writer and art director. He eventually got married and never missed mine or my sisters' birthday parties. On Christmas Eve, he put on a Santa costume and stood waving on our front lawn while my sisters and I, all in our pyjamas, leaned against the living room windows gasping (and me, crying).

Then there were the other periods when Mike was in and out of the hospital, especially near the end of his life. He began showing up to our birthday dinners with an oxygen tank in tow, his signature phlegmy cough worsening.

Mike had to endure so much suffering, and I imagine his body never felt like a safe place for him to be. Just living required planning, maintenance, gruelling sacrifice, and heavy uncertainty. If Mike's illness taught our family anything, it was to appreciate the gift of time. From the moment Mike was born, he was aware of his limited years, and because of that, he had no patience for wasted time — a merciless clock ticked loudly in his ears. Mike suffered no fools, lived how he wanted, and hated if anyone was late.

This perspective on time is a gift we never asked for but were handed when Mike decided he couldn't go on at thirty-seven. It was a loss so abnormal and heartbreaking, the effects will be carried with us forever.

And eventually, all those years ago, the loudest voice in my head was one scolding me for wasting valuable days.

One life, wasted months, lost hours.

Precious minutes spent like loose change.

It was summer again, but this time the Toronto heat was different. A fire had been lit. My life was evolving in a way that no longer held space for Reed, edged out by new friends, new routines, and returning self-respect. Blake and I were spending every day together, even getting jobs at the same downtown bar. She was my best friend. My sister. She didn't know specific details of what I was dealing with behind closed doors, but she was always supportive and warm when my mental health took a nosedive for *seemingly* no reason. I knew she really loved me. And without her knowledge, she was also resuscitating me.

One day as we walked down a crowded city sidewalk, Blake asked, "Are you sure you're okay? You seem sad today."

"I just haven't heard from Reed in a while. I'm not sure where he is. He does this sometimes."

"He's not answering his phone?"

"His phone has been off for days. I went to his apartment but no answer. Who knows."

Although I tried my best to downplay it, Reed missing was all I could think about, mostly out of habit.

"You know that's not normal, right? That is not normal behaviour for a boyfriend. You can't just disappear if you've chosen to have a girlfriend. No one's making him be in a relationship, and you kind of give up your right to vanish." I knew she was right.

Blake was a fluorescent reminder there were concerts to go to, bars to drink in, friends to meet, dance floors to hit, pools to break into, people to flirt with, and parties to crash. She reminded me it was okay to make my own choices, and her confidence was infectious. Boldness poured from her, and I was benefiting thanks to sheer proximity.

Blake gave me the invaluable gift of not seeing me through the eyes of my relationship with Reed and my deteriorating mental health. I felt those in my life had started to see me only as depressed, self-destructive, and stuck in a toxic relationship. But Blake never treated me that way. She recognized the strength in me when I didn't see it in myself.

The year before, Reed "jokingly" told me in front of our friends that I "should be bulimic." Blake's self-assurance, joy, and total confidence was like a cleanse.

She had this way of turning everyone around her into family, gathering strays wherever she went, making up a group of crazy, tattooed, fun, confident, devilishly rebellious misfits. She was brilliant, fiercely kind, razor sharp, and could outshine and outwit anyone. Everyone who met Blake became obsessed with her — her attention felt extra special — and she'd chosen me.

She was also a rebel. A true rebel. A rebel who had no time for this "boyfriend" (who she'd never even met) being the reason I usually couldn't come up a few floors to her party. (There were nights Reed would, in a roundabout way, ask me to send him a photo to prove that I was, in fact, in my own apartment and not upstairs with her and Logan.) B was a rebel who had no time for an early night in. A rebel who had zero time for someone making me feel small — not when there was fun to be had.

Now I had a pitbull in my corner.

Blake and I had just finished a late shift at the bar.

"You're coming, right? You're coming," Blake said as we changed out of our uniforms. Logan was the bartender at a restaurant next door. Once her shifts were finished, she would go over and sit with him while he worked.

"I don't know . . . I don't think so. Maybe." I glanced at my phone waiting for a response from Reed. If he wanted to hang out I would probably go, again, mostly out of habit.

"Are you seeing Reed tonight?" She looked at me out of the corner of her icy-blue eyes. I felt a pang of embarrassment.

"I still haven't heard from him," I checked my phone again.

"Don't tell me he's still MIA."

"No, I don't think so. He's probably working or something," I lied.

"Well then, hang out with us. He can come to you if he wants to see you. For once. Come get a drink," she said as she zipped up her knee-high Dr. Martens. "Or tell him to come. I'd like meet him, finally."

Blake reminded me of how I used to be, back when I was self-assured and independent. Before Reed squeezed out every last drop of confidence from me like a wet rag.

"Okay, sure. I'll come. He isn't answering me anyway." I threw my phone into my purse.

The thought of Reed being angry about where I was or who I was with was becoming too exhausting to worry about. I was starting to detach, and one by one, cut the knots he'd tied so tight. It was a strange, liberating, and equally sad time. On one hand, I was being handed a second chance at my early twenties. On the other hand, I was harbouring immense grief. Letting him go was going to sting.

My life was in a time of nerve-racking, unsettling, wildly exciting transition. I was breaking free from Reed's control, his disapproving voice fading in my mind. Finally, the anxiety he caused began to plague my nerves less.

One weekend shortly after, Marley and I lay shoulder to shoulder on the carpeted floor of her cousins' basement and I said, "I don't think I want to be with him anymore. I think I'm done. It just doesn't *feel* good."

"Good!" She practically yelled. It was bursting with relief but free from judgment.

Reed had nearly torn me and Marley's relationship apart. Unable to take the highs and lows that came with me being his girlfriend, Marley eventually told me if I didn't end my relationship, she would have no choice but to move out.

"I'm sorry, Cal. But if you continue to see him, I can't live here anymore. It's too hard to watch, and it's starting to take a real toll on me, too. I can't do it anymore." She told me one day as we stood at either end of our apartment's narrow hallway.

My body turned to warm Jell-O as I pretended to puff out my chest.

"Okay, well if that's what you want to do, then you should move out." My outsides projected anger and resentment, that she was wrong, overreacting. But my insides were jittery with panic, unsure of where I would live, and with who. Fear filled me as I wondered if now I was truly alone with him.

"It isn't what I *want* to do, but I don't really think I have a choice. Your relationship is just so toxic and I can't watch you sit in a dark room all day. You might not know because I've been trying to hide it, but it's starting to affect me."

There was no way of defending myself. She was right. Of course she was right.

Marley moved out. We wrote the building a letter letting them know we were terminating our lease and signed it in silence.

We divided up the clothes we shared, packed up our once happy, light apartment into boxes — separately, so we didn't have to see each other — and I moved into a brand-new condo with my younger sister. That weekend away, lying on the basement floor, was the first real time Marley and I had spent together in months. I saw the good I was missing. With Marley, I was safe and free of guilt. The way life used to feel.

Back in the city, I knew what I had to do; I was ready to end my relationship one final time. No hesitation. I wasn't in love with him anymore, not the way I used to be. His face, I used to examine; his words, I used to store. They no longer fed me. I had sacrificed too much, drifting so far out of reach, any further and I wasn't sure I was ever going to get myself back. I was sad, bitter, and destructive. I knew I had a disappearing window of opportunity to reverse the damage.

I have trouble placing when exactly it happened or how soon it was after Marley and I lay on the floor, but one day shortly after, I decided to do it.

The city was dark and quiet. Numb, I stood outside my condo on Bay Street, waiting for a cab to pass by. I didn't tell anyone what I was doing. This was for me.

On the way over, I planned what I would say and prepared myself for his heartbreaking indifference — the indifference I knew all too well. I mentally suited up in armour for his utter disinterest in losing me. It was still his weapon of choice and it always managed to cut me off at the knees.

As I stepped foot into Reed's apartment, I felt just a little bit of my confidence melt away. I knew this world — our world — so well. There were things we'd experienced within those four walls that no one else could ever understand. Memories only he and I knew existed. Suddenly, I wasn't so sure I was ready to walk away. Was I really okay with another girl in this apartment, holding his hand, sleeping in his bed? I'd loved him since the day I saw him. Was I okay with someone standing where I once stood?

But this wasn't just for me. Each time I found myself inside the suffocating walls of Reed's apartment, I lost a little bit more of my healthy relationships outside of Reed — was pushed further from the people who made me feel good about my interests, the ones who would sit outside with me for hours if I was anxious, the ones who would never hurt me the way Reed had. This wasn't love, it was abuse. I was already emotionally one foot out the door. So, eventually, I mustered up every ounce of confidence I had left, braced for how sad I was about to make myself, and said, "I don't want to do this anymore. You've hurt me too many times. I'm done."

We were standing in the middle of his studio apartment. He stared back at me for a moment, then said, "Okay, I think you're probably right."

It was the exact indifference I was prepared for. Part of me wanted to stay, unable to accept that this was the last time I was ever going to be in his apartment, wanting to savour my last few seconds as his girlfriend. But my gut told me it was time to leave. Enough now. I'd given too much, lost too much; my confidence, my body, my best friend, my ability to feel happy. It was now or never.

I took a few steps to the front door and knelt to tie my shoes.

Suddenly, Reed's feet appeared next to mine. He stood tall above me as I crouched beneath his shadow. My heart began to thump against my ribs, and as I fiddled with my shoelaces, he spat on me.

"Seriously?" I rolled my eyes and wiped his spit off my shoulder.

It wasn't the indifference I expected, but it was anger I recognized. I stood up and reached for my purse. He was planted between me and the door. As I reached for the door handle, he took one step backwards and pushed his body weight against it, holding it firmly shut.

"I'm leaving. Let me open the door," I told him, doing my best to conceal any fear. He didn't utter one word back. He remained still, chin tilted toward the ceiling, eyes vacant. I tried again, but he didn't budge. My insides began to shiver.

Sometimes, when my dogs both have food and one moves a little bit too close to the other, they get into a standoff. One foot apart, they stare at each other, ready to pounce. Over time, I've learned the absolute worst thing I can do is swoop in and snatch one of them up. Any sudden movement and it's on; they go after each other, teeth out. That's how this moment felt. If I made any sudden movement, he'd pounce.

With a measured, firm voice, I tried to talk to him, tried to reason with him, as I had before when he was beginning to scare me.

"I know this is hard. I know it feels terrible. It does for me, too. But I have to go now. You know I do. We can't do this anymore. You have to let me go."

My heart continued to thump, then it got worse; I remembered I hadn't told anyone where I was. No one was waiting up for me, no one was going to make sure I got home safely, no one was checking their phone. Not one person knew I was with him in that moment, and it was getting late. That realization forced my body to launch into survival mode. I pounced. Out of desperation, I tried to shove him out of the way with all my body weight and grab the door handle. But he barely moved. He was much stronger than I was. I grabbed the door handle with both hands and tried pulling it open. He stared at me — expressionless — as I did everything in my power to break free.

Then he lunged again, just as he had lunged at me before.

Reed picked me up and threw me backwards like a doll onto the bed, his heavier body landing on top of mine. I struggled and fought to get out from underneath him while he held me down by the arms. It was a familiar move, but this time it felt different. When he'd tossed me onto the bed before, I didn't know why he was angry, what he was trying to accomplish, what message he was trying to send. This time, I knew; he wasn't going to let me leave him.

Still holding my purse, I wiggled out from underneath him, sprang back onto my feet, and made another dash for the front door. But once again, he picked me up and launched me backwards onto his bed. It happened a third time. This time, when I hit the bed with his body on top of mine, he began to erratically grab at my clothes, attempting to pull them off as I struggled and braced myself to be raped.

"What are you doing?" I yelled, batting away his grabby, aggressive hands as they flew across my body.

Calm and measured, his low voice whispered into my ear, "Just giving you what you want."

The weight of his body alone was enough to make it hard to breathe, his desire for control crushing my lungs once again. I managed to wiggle free and made yet another run for the door. But once again, he beat me to it and stood blocking my exit. I was trapped.

I don't know how long it lasted, but we continued this dance for what felt like hours. He refused to let me go, but I kept trying. What else could I do.

My mind raced. *Can I somehow get to my cell phone? Maybe I can make it to the bathroom, lock the door, and then call 911? If I call 911, will he kill me? Should I just start screaming? Maybe it hasn't come to that yet.* In his calmer moments, I tried communicating: "You have to let me go." "Why are you doing this to me?" "You have to just let me go. We can't be together anymore."

Then I simply tried to open the door again, moving slowly so as not to spook him, and for whatever reason, he inexplicably stepped aside. The smug look on his face told me it was a trap, but I chose to take the bait. My body was getting too tired to keep fighting.

Reed's apartment was at the opposite end of the hallway from the building's elevators. It was late, and it seemed no one else on the floor was awake. There was no activity from behind the neighbouring doors. I prayed I would run into someone in the hallway or the elevator. I just needed one other person — one witness, anyone — and it could mean me getting out of the building alive.

My walk was contained but rushed down the dimly lit hallway. I worried if I ran, he would run after me, like a wounded animal trying not to draw attention. In the elevator, I began pressing the button over and over, as quickly as my shaking fingers would allow.

I knew he'd be after me.

As the noisy elevator doors began to creak slowly shut, like a cliché scene in a movie, he snuck through just before the bang of the metal doors closing. My heart dropped. Empty, yet pulsing with adrenaline, my brain oscillated between fear of the reality I was facing and next to no fear whatsoever. Instead, anger propelled me forward, fuelled by this person with whom I'd shared so many good moments, now forcing me to literally run away. I was angry he thought he could scare me — angry he thought he could bully me into not leaving him. Then the next moment, I was nothing but scared again.

When the elevator reached the ground floor, I rushed past him toward the front door of the building. His eyes pierced the back of my head.

Breathing outside air was a relief; there were times, just moments before, I wasn't sure I would ever see outside of those four walls again. But it was late and the street was empty. I turned in the direction of a major intersection, and walked quickly down the deserted sidewalk. Reed followed closely, telling me I was a disappointment.

The intersection I hoped would be busy was instead ominous and dead — nothing but the occasional car, until miraculously, a cab approached. I threw a desperate hand in the air and it stopped just in front of me. I ran around to the other side of the car. From a safe distance, I looked Reed in the eye and told him, "Take one more step toward me and I'll scream." I stepped into the cab and shut the door behind me.

As we drove away, I spun around and watched Reed begin to leisurely walk back toward his apartment.

The cab made its way through the quiet streets of Toronto. I tried to slow my breathing and heart rate. At least, for the moment, I was safe. Reed knew the area where I just moved, but he didn't know the details. He'd never find me. Thankfully, even before that night, I'd had the foresight to lie about my address and floor number.

Ten minutes later, I unlocked the door to my empty, dark apartment. My sister was at her boyfriend's. Our place still smelled like paint and plastic, not yet seeped in the smell of our furniture and clothes. I climbed into bed and eventually, somehow, fell asleep. It never crossed my mind to call the police.

I woke up the next morning with salty skin. Outside, it poured rain. An endless line of traffic inched its way through the city below on dark, wet pavement. Droplets filled my bedroom window, blurring the line of distant red brake lights. I stayed in bed, riddled with anxiety and panic, suddenly nauseated by the height of my condo's windows. I called a friend.

She answered, "Hey!"

"Hey, what are you doing?" I asked her.

"Literally nothing. Watching TV. What's up?"

"I'm so anxious today. I don't know why. I can't seem to calm down. Can you come over and keep me company?"

"Yeah sure. I'll throw some clothes on and walk over."

We lay around all day. I never told her what happened only twelve hours earlier. I'm not sure I was even thinking about it. The memory already felt distant and out of reach, like a story I'd heard, not one I witnessed myself. I was frozen, curled up in my soft bed in a state of hardened panic with no desire or thought to share.

When I think back on myself in the weeks immediately after, I see a girl struggling to know who she is yet having more fun than she'd been previously allowed. A young girl given a second chance and a fresh start, but who was thin, frail, and gaunt, who had a lifeless complexion and was losing her hair. I see a young girl dressing only in clothes she thought would make her attractive and outwardly confident, not someone who could be taken advantage of. I see someone wanting anyone else's attention other than Reed, while terrified of all men. I see someone lost, in pain, trying to forget. I see someone trying to find their old confidence, finally pulling their shoulders back and lifting their chin. I see someone ready to take up some space again. I see someone sad.

My memory of the weeks around that night feel foggy. It's something I'm hesitant to say. *She doesn't even remember. Victims don't forget.* I've seen comments like these directed at women whose memories are occasionally fuzzy due to the intensity. I feel like I should be able to rehash every moment down to the nanosecond in order to be believed. I can't. Not when it comes to these weeks. But I know what he did — what happened after that night, how long it was until I saw him next, when I finally blocked his phone number, when I cut off all contact — these things aren't as clear.

Instead, I floated around trying to push through my every day, trying to keep myself alive, trying to move forward without wanting to die. When I reflect on this time, it barely feels like it was me who existed inside of myself. It feels more like someone else's story, someone I don't know very well who only shared pieces.

I didn't realize what he was doing.

CHAPTER 19

One week after escaping Reed's apartment, I sat next to my friend Laine at my parents' kitchen island, scrolling Facebook.

"Here's the guy I was talking about," I turned my laptop to face her. It was a bright, sunny day. The windows were open, 70s on 7 was playing, as it always does at my parents' house.

"So you worked with him last summer?" Laine asked, scanning his album of profile pictures.

"Yeah, I didn't think anything of it at the time, obviously. But he's cute, no?"

His name was Stephen. We met at the restaurant where I'd worked the summer before when Reed and I had been otherwise inseparable. Stephen was four years older than me, and I'd always taken comfort in his maturity. He had a big smile, nice teeth, and small hoop earrings. Stephen was a bartender; I'd been a hostess. On the hottest of summer days when I was working the patio, he would pop out of the side door balancing trays of Aperol Spritzes and mint mojitos. As I looked through his photos, the summer before replayed in my mind: passing each other in slow motion, me in a tight black dress — which he would eventually comment on a year after the fact, and his smile making guests fall in love.

"Are you going to message him?" Laine asked, pulling my attention back.

"You think I should? What should I say?" I opened the message tab.

"Do it! Do it. Who fucking cares if he doesn't want to hang out. Who cares, honestly. Just give it a shot." Laine had a way of making everything feel wonderfully low risk. Small. Insignificant in the grand scheme of life. *It could be way fucking worse, Callie*, she'd always say.

"Okay. How's this? Is this dumb?" I turned my laptop toward her. My message read: *Hey! It's been a while. How are you? I was wondering if you wanted to grab a drink sometime.* Short, sweet, to the point. And also, evidently, effective.

It was purely speculation, but to me, Stephen seemed like a "good guy." A reliable guy. One that all women would be safe around, drunk or sober, happy or sad. Making the first move was new to me, something fear of rejection had previously made too risky, but things were different now. I carried with me a secret confidence. Reed left me feeling invincible, with a set of steely armour. This wasn't two years ago when I had no experience, when I could be easily hurt and didn't know the rules. I walked away from my last relationship with an understanding that left me wise beyond my years, carrying the baggage of someone three times my age. Now, I was the scary one. I was the one who was untouchable, unflinching, complicated. I wouldn't bat an eye at childish games like an unanswered text. I wouldn't be shocked or impressed by mediocre skills in bed. I was experienced and knowledgeable. Reed's intention to wreck me instead left me unflappable.

Plus, compared to the pain of losing Reed the way I had, nothing would hurt.

I was craving new, believing it was the only way to rinse my mouth of the last few years. And although I would have never admitted it, nor could I see it, I was searching for someone to do my healing for me, and I set my sights on Stephen.

He wrote back: *Hey Callie! It's so nice to hear from you. I'd love to grab a drink. Let me know when you're free. Maybe this weekend?*

Although it seemed fast, I marvelled at how quickly I seemed to be moving on and forgetting. It was a sliver of relief, and I wasn't willing to question it.

It would be a few years until I understood the real meaning of the word "trauma."

After my shift one night, soon after, I crossed the street and threw my purse up onto the bar.

"Hey! Hi! So nice to see you!" Stephen made his way around the counter and gave me a warm hug. "I'm almost done. Can I get you something to drink in the meantime?"

I felt the butterflies in my stomach quiet. Stephen was sweet, and there was something about the way he talked, comforting and familiar, as if he hovered above all the insecurities I had, all the drama which had engulfed my life over the last few years, all the disappearances and attacks that had been hurled. Stephen was an adult.

Everything passes. Nothing hurts forever.

CHAPTER 20

The bar where Blake and I worked had two big patios and was a very popular spot in the city that summer. Still, with little industry experience, I remained a hostess.

It was a few hours into an afternoon shift when Reed sat himself on the street-level patio. Just a few weeks earlier, I told him this was over. And yet, there he was, welcoming himself into my new life and my new routine.

The sun was shining, but my eyes saw nothing but black. I stormed over to him.

I wanted to scream. "What are you doing here?"

He said, "I just want to be close to you." And paused. "Have you been hanging out with any of your old friends from across the street?" Reed gestured to the restaurant where I'd worked the summer before when I spent every night with his arms around me.

Reed had no way of knowing about Stephen. We'd only been on a few casual dates. No photos were being posted (plus, Reed wasn't even on social media). I figured he might be watching me, following me down the street. There was absolutely no other way he'd know.

But I wasn't doing anything wrong, and I wasn't about to be intimidated.

So, I said, "Yes. I have," and stared back at him. I told him, "You have to go," turned around and went back inside. Back at the hostess stand, I felt a shiver run down my spine. My body was ready for a fight, my armpits tingling with sweat. He wasn't going to leave my life quietly.

Another day not long after, he showed up again. This time, he walked in through the front door.

"You must be kidding me, Reed. What are you doing here?"

"I know, I know. I'll go. I just wanted to give you these. I thought you might like them." He reached into his pocket and pulled out colourful yarn bracelets just like the ones he wore. I always loved how they looked tied around his boney wrist. This was a whole other side of Reed I didn't know. My expectations were founded on his utter indifference, weaponized to keep me off-balance.

"Okay, thanks. You can go now." I carelessly placed the bracelets on the hostess stand and looked back at him. "You can't show up here anymore, okay?"

Reed smiled.

Although a smug part of me was enjoying this newfound desperation, I was getting nervous. I strongly believed he'd been following me, and I often worked late, then walked home alone, some nights after two a.m. But I was determined not to let him affect my new routine or scare me into anything. Years had already been wasted as his puppet.

One afternoon before another shift, Blake and I were sitting in the locker room when my phone rang. It was a number I didn't recognize.

I answered, "Hello?"

"Hey. We need to talk."

"Who is this?"

"It's Reed."

I'd blocked his number. "Whose number is this?"

"I got a new one."

I hung up. A couple minutes later, I got yet another call from yet another phone number. I shouldn't have answered, but there was a part of me that felt special now that he was chasing.

". . . Hello."

"Can we please talk?"

I blocked both numbers and soon changed my own.

Then Reed showed up for a third time.

It was a sunny afternoon in August, and I was working the patio shift. The sidewalk was busy, as it always is when Toronto is hot. I kept an eye out for Stephen, who would occasionally pop out onto the patio across the street with a tray of icy drinks.

I'd been at work for a couple hours when I saw Reed rounding the corner. Even though he'd been top of mind and he'd already shown up twice, I was somehow still surprised to see his face somewhere that felt completely separate from the world we once shared. This wasn't a part of the city where we'd spent time. My brain was no longer consumed by our life together.

Coming toward me were familiar dark eyes, expressionless as they always were when he was about to get angry or hurt me. As he moved closer, I wondered if I should run inside. I didn't know what Reed wanted or what he was capable of, but his feet were determined. As he took his last steps toward me, I thought about how I'd blocked his number and how he seemed to know I was dating someone new. While my mind raced, adding up all the reasons I knew he was dangerously angry with me, I stood still, refusing to be threatened by him any longer. My life had moved on, and I wasn't about to cower away from this person I knew so well. I wasn't about to cower away from anything.

Instead, I braced myself.

And at the very last moment, a brief flash of panic rushed through my mind: *Is he going to stab me?*

Reed pushed one headphone off his ear. Then he lunged, gripping me tightly with one hand, clawing the back of my head, while the other gripped my waist. He pushed his lips against mine with rage, and I threw my hands up onto his face, thrashing my head from side to side to shake myself free. He held me tight in his grasp.

My back arched from the sheer force of his body launching into mine. With both hands on his face, I eventually pushed him off. Then, without a word, he turned around and walked away, hands casually in his pockets. I stood with my hand over my mouth, frozen and silent. My waist and the back of my head, where his angry hands had been, began to ache just as they had many times before. Once again, he'd used my body just the way he wanted — this time claiming ownership on a public stage — and left me alone to pick up the pieces.

I was unaware of this moment's gravity. I had no idea it would change the course of everything and that those ten seconds would be our last chapter.

Although I was rattled by what he'd chosen to do in broad daylight, on a busy street, at my place of work, what he physically did that day was small on the scale of what he'd already done. Aggression from him wasn't new and it wasn't the worst I'd experienced at his hands. Not by any stretch. So, I was confused when, minutes later, the manager called me to her office and said she had no choice but to call the police.

"Call the *police*? Why? I'm fine, really. I appreciate it, I do, but I'm totally fine."

It wasn't adding up. Yes, I was caught off guard that he put his hands on me in public (and that no one around stepped in to help). But of all the times to involve the police, this wasn't it.

The manager explained that because it was an assault that took place on their premises, she had no choice but to report it.

"Assault?" I looked at her, confused.

"Yes, and one on the bar's premises, so my hands are tied here. I wanted to let you know," she said.

"But what are they going to do?"

"I'm not sure," she told me.

"I really, really don't think this is necessary. I don't want to make this a bigger deal than it needs to be."

The manager sighed and said, "I'm sorry, Callie. I'll let you know when they're here."

Assault was never a word I considered using for the violence we experienced together. At least, never out loud. He couldn't possibly have assaulted me when I knew him as well as I did. Wasn't that a word reserved for strangers who are attacked on the subway or on a quiet, dark street? Not this person whose toothbrush I'd used and whose clothes I'd slept in. Not this person who was deeply important to me, who my friends had also loved, who'd brushed the hair out of my face, and who sent me home with curated playlists.

But something changed once I left the manager's office; I became increasingly shaken with every minute that passed. I started to cry, which didn't happen often, and ran around the bar frantically.

"Does anyone know where Blake is? Where is Blake?" My eyes were wide with stress, and I couldn't focus.

Blake ran down the stairs and threw her arms around me. "What happened? They said Reed showed up again? Are you okay?"

I cried harder into her shoulder.

"I swear to God, if I see that guy . . . What a fucking loser." Blake's eyes were extra icy that day.

Up until then, I'd felt safe in public, but that was no longer true.

The manager — a virtual stranger — throwing labels around felt violating. She didn't know us; she didn't know our relationship. She couldn't possibly understand that I loved him, and he loved me. How dare she. This was the first time anyone other than the two of us had caught a glimpse of what was happening behind our tightly closed door. Our secrets were spilling out onto the sidewalk as I ran in circles trying to collect them. I didn't want anyone to act on what they'd seen. Reed and I used to be trapped in a toxic cycle, but it was over now. No one needed to get involved. I had already handled it.

I stepped outside to call my parents who were away on vacation. Not too long after, the police arrived to take me to the station.

I want out.

CHAPTER 21

The front of the police station was lined with cold, plastic chairs. Uncomfortable, I sat rocking my weight back and forth with crossed arms and folded ankles. My phone vibrated in my hand. *Let me know how it goes and if you need anything.* Blake wrote. *I love you.* My eyes darted around the police station. It was quieter than I expected one would be downtown Toronto, in a city of three million people. We were right in the thick of it — surrounded by restaurants, bars, and universities — and yet, the station was calm. Nothing but the occasional desk phone ringing or a passing officer.

The front door opened abruptly, and Marley appeared beside me.

"Hey. How are you?" She asked, sitting down next to me. "What *happened*?"

"Thanks for coming. Sorry to call you like that. I don't even know if there's a point in you being here. I don't know what's about to happen or what they'll need from me." I looked back at her, but all I could see were the two officers ten feet away, talking.

"It's okay, I want to be here. Can you tell me what happened?" She looked at me deeply.

"Yeah, um," I tried to remember. "He showed up at the bar again, which was the third time, and he kissed me really aggressively. He grabbed me hard and then forced his lips onto mine, kind of violently, and I tried to push him off. Then he just walked away again."

"I'm so sorry." She shook her head lightly. "Did he say anything?"

"Nothing. I don't think he said anything. He just walked up to me, pushed his face onto mine and then left, like he was marking his territory or something." I felt almost dumb recounting it to Marley. It was hardly an event.

"Then what happened? Did you call the police?"

"No, no. I wouldn't have called them. My manager did. She said she kind of had to. I don't want them involved, really. I don't want things to get worse," I lowered my voice and my eyes. "I don't want him to be in trouble or for this to become a big thing. I'm fine. We aren't together anymore, and I just need to move on."

Just then, an officer approached us.

"Okay, Callie, we're ready for you, if you want to come with us," he said.

"What do you need from her? What does she have to do?" Marley asked.

"We need to hear what happened and get a little bit more information. It shouldn't be too long."

I stood up and looked back at Marley. "Okay, see you in a bit."

Detective Liu led me into a small room, and we sat on either side of a desk. In front of us was a video camera.

"Okay, so we're recording. Time right now is 8:30 p.m." He began. "Can you state your name, please?"

"Callie O'Reilly."

I wondered if he was annoyed by me and my boyfriend troubles, wasting his time in a city where real crimes were happening.

I'd changed out of my uniform and was now in a black T-shirt dress. I tugged on the end, willing it to miraculously grow a few inches longer to cover more of my cold, pale thighs.

Next, a Commissioner of Oaths entered the room and reminded me that lying was a serious criminal offence. "Do you, Callie O'Reilly, solemnly affirm that the evidence that you shall give in this investigation shall be the truth, the whole truth, and nothing but the truth?"

"I do."

Detective Liu put his pen to paper and asked, "How did you guys meet?"

My mind flooded with memories: love, loss, pain, heartbreak, fear. How do I tell our story? Our real story, not the one I'd been selling.

I told him, "We used to live on the same block, and we met at a bar near both of our apartments."

"Do you want to explain how you guys started dating?"

I took a breath and turned back time. Back through the good days and the bad, through countless hours and monotonous minutes. I let my mind go right back to the beginning, to when I first saw him.

In my mind, I'm tiptoeing up the fire escape, door propped open an inch. He's in sock feet with messy hair, and he smells of incense. Warm sun floods the room, and suddenly, it's scorching July. He knocks on my door, skateboard in hand, and kisses me on the forehead. I'm surrounded by the blue walls, running across the creaky floor and down the rusty fire escape. He runs his hands through his hair and winks from across the room. I remember him. I remember I loved him. Love him. We face each other in bed, and he tells me he'll never love anyone else the same way.

I stare forward and let myself feel it. The nooks and crannies I'd previously buried — the truths I'd somehow twisted and excused — and let go of the lies I'd been telling myself.

In my mind, his hands are around my throat and my pulse throbs from my neck, pressure growing in my head. He smacks a drink from my hands, pink splatters covering the walls. My skull is aching, my heart racing. I squirm to break free. He strikes my back, my skin stinging. His fingertips dig into my waist, his lips forced on mine. Bruised and tender, I'm pushing, pleading, running; he's following.

A story almost impossible to tell was somehow packed into a complete story with a beginning, a middle, and now, an end. We met, fell in love, and broke up just like everyone else.

I wondered how I was sounding to the officer, if he believed me, if he felt bad for me, as he looked at me like a lost teen who'd run away from home.

I'd been too overwhelmed to ask about the repercussions of me spilling the details of our time together. Or maybe I did ask. I can't remember.

I talked, and time passed. I tried to make out Detective Liu's upside-down scribbles.

Finally, he asked, "Is there anything else you would like to add?"

"I think he is depressed or has some sort of mental health issue. He's unstable."

"Okay, I will end the interview here." Detective Liu spun around and ended the recording.

The next thing I remember, he tells me, "Well, Callie, based on what we've heard today, we are going to charge him with the following: four counts of assault, one count of criminal harassment, one count of sexual assault, and one count of forcible confinement." He looked back at me, not expectantly, which I was grateful for. He was giving me space to digest. "Do you have any questions for me?"

"What does the last one mean?"

"Forcible confinement?"

"Yes."

"Yes, good question. Forcible confinement basically means holding someone against their will. So when he wouldn't allow you to leave his apartment." Calm but firm. He was sure.

"I see. Okay." I took a long pause.

"Do you have any other questions?"

I tried to think quickly through molasses.

"I don't know. I guess I'm just wondering what happens now. Is he going to jail?"

Jail.

"Well, we've already arrested Reed, and he's on his way to the station right now. We will most likely hold him overnight."

Panic washed over me for the first time. "He's coming here right now?" I stood up, legs yearning for the front door, wanting to grab Marley and run.

"Yes, Reed is on his way here."

I pictured the police showing up at Reed's front door, the hands that hurt me behind his back, a small smirk on his face, as if being proved right; he was not built for this world. He was a misunderstood alien, and it was everyone else that was the problem.

"Do I have to see him?" I became more panicked with each word.

"No, definitely not. We will make *sure* you don't see him. That would be dangerous, and we won't let it happen. He'll be in a whole other part of the building."

"Okay. Good. Good." The air was thick, and I struggled to take a deep breath.

I remember the next part like this. "Callie, it's important you understand that you will not be charging Reed. He's being charged by the police, not by you. It is a requirement in Ontario that if there is a suspected crime of domestic abuse, the police must lay charges. Does that make sense?"

"So I won't have to be involved at all?"

"Well, not necessarily. We will have to see how he pleads."

Victim. Pleads. Arrested. Jail. Assault. Had I been assaulted? Even worse, had I been sexually assaulted? A police officer seemed to think so. I'd never thought of myself in those terms, and now, somehow, a label sought to change everything.

Eventually, the detective opened the door and across the lobby, Marley sprang to her feet. "How did it go? Are you okay?"

"Yeah, I'm okay. It was okay. I think. Reed is on his way here, so I want to leave." I turned back toward Detective Liu. "Can I leave?"

"You can. Do you two want a ride back?"

I looked at Marley. "I have to go back to work. I have to pick up my things. Do you want to come with me?"

"Sure," Marley said as she threw her purse over her shoulder. "Why is he on his way here?"

I looked at Marley, eyes wide, "They arrested him."

Marley's face revealed nothing. She put a hand on my back, and we made our way to the front doors.

Marley and I climbed into the back seat of the police car in silence, waiting to be alone to have a real conversation. My lungs were tight, like an elastic band was wrapped around my chest. I took my cell phone out of my purse and glanced at messages from Blake, my parents, my sisters, Stephen, and put it face down on my lap. Reed was officially the villain of my story, and this time I couldn't hide it. I was no longer able to protect him from himself. I knew he didn't deserve the help, but the habit was nearly impossible to break. I shielded Reed, I lied, I sugar coated everything, I snuck around, and I stuck around. How could I suddenly allow a spotlight to shine on the truth?

"I'm just going to grab my things, then go home," I told Marley as we swayed through the city.

"Okay," she looked over at me. "I'm going to go home then, but call me if you need anything. I mean it, okay?"

"Okay. Thank you for coming. I'm sorry." I paused. "For everything."

Back at the bar, I emptied my locker. It was late and the hot sun had faded. Blake sat next to me for a brief moment before I left. "I'm here for you, however you need it. And let me tell you, if I see that fucking guy . . ." she practically yelled. I knew she meant it. Next to Blake, I was safe.

"You know . . . I don't think I am going to go home yet. I don't want to just sit there alone," I said. "Is Logan working? Maybe I'll wait there for Stephen."

"Yeah, I think he's on the patio. Go sit with him," she nodded emphatically.

"Okay, I think I will. I'm assuming you're going there whenever you get cut?"

"Yeah, so I'll see you there. If you stay that long."

I sat at Logan's bar and watched as he threw shakers and bottles of vodka in the air, making various drinks, laughing, and joking with coworkers and customers. He brought me my favourite pasta dish and a couple drinks on the house. Finally, after an hour, Stephen appeared next to me.

"Wow. What *happened*? I saw the cops. Are you okay?" He looked at me with worried eyebrows.

"He came by again and . . . just . . . grabbed me, I guess. It's okay." I didn't feel like talking about it anymore. "Logan's been taking care of me! What do you want to drink?"

Logan appeared in front of us. "Hey man," they shook hands. "What can I get you?"

"Hey, I'll take a Barking Squirrel, thanks." Stephen's smile faded as he turned back to me. "Do you want to talk about it?"

Stephen and I sat at the bar for a couple of hours, watching tables fill up, then empty. I shared only a little about what happened and even less about how I felt. My thoughts, my feelings, my life was no longer for sharing.

"Shall we?" He said and stood up from the bar stool. "How are you getting home?"

"I guess, walking," I said, staring down the busy sidewalk with dread. "Did you drive?"

"Yeah, do you want a lift?" He'd only had a beer or two.

"That would be great, actually. Thanks."

In the passenger seat of Stephen's car, a city plastered with

Reed's face was wiped clean. Just for a moment. I directed Stephen's turns as he blasted a screamy heavy metal band.

Looking at Stephen I said, "This music is crazy! You really like it?"

He glanced over at me, enormous smile on his face. "What's not to like?"

"It's so overwhelming! And scary!"

Stephen laughed. The screaming vocals didn't match his sweetness. His gentleness. His kindness.

We reached the one-way street next to my condo, Stephen slowed the car, and I unclipped my seatbelt. My body was buzzed like I'd had too much caffeine. The thought of walking into my empty apartment, sleeping alone, thinking about Reed, filled me with threatening darkness. I knew what it would look like: listening to music he liked, looking at photos of him, and hating myself. He needed to be erased. So, I dove in headfirst.

"Want to come up and meet Dex?" I looked at him over my shoulder, one hand on the door handle.

Stephen paused, most likely running through the details of my day, the ones I'd shared with him. Most likely wondering what the right answer was, what the kind answer was, or what he was potentially getting himself into.

Finally, he said, "Sure. I'll come up for a bit."

Eleven floors up, I kissed Stephen. With equal force, I was flooded by sickness and relief. The wheels were really coming off now, and I could feel every bump. A desperate desire to erase Reed was dictating my choices, and my brain knew better. This wasn't the way to do it. I feared men, I feared Stephen, even though I knew better there too. My judgment couldn't be trusted, not with a grown man standing in front of me. An old version of me believed Stephen was a good person, but my vision had been compromised and I couldn't be sure.

Erase. Erase. Replace. This is the only way he'll go away for good. This is the only way he won't come back.

Once Stephen left, I sat still on my bed without turning on any lights and felt a pit in my stomach heavier than I'd ever felt. Loneliness and pain washed over me. Reed was gone. He was gone for good. I'd done it, gotten rid of him and told the truth. I'd done what I needed to do to protect myself.

That day at the police station, I didn't touch on the sexual violence I'd experienced. I could have shared so much more; which I assume could have have led to even more charges. But it took years to see what happened between us in our most intimate moments for what it was. Sitting in front of the detective, a man many years older than me, I silenced a piece of me that had more to say, quieted by shame, embarrassment, and deep uncertainty. Instead, I focused on what I thought was indisputable and simply easier to explain. I thought by doing that I was doing a "good job," providing police with the information they needed, not the experiences I couldn't even understand myself. I worried if the police caught a whiff of any uncertainty, things could go sideways.

I wish, for the sake of young women, I'd told the police more. It was my chance to utilize this experience and take advantage of a rare opportunity in front of me. I was sitting with a police officer, with evidence of abuse, being listened to.

Maybe I've spent the last decade trying to find a voice for the sexual trauma, to warn other women and share my experience as a way to measure their own.

I will always remember you as the guy who taught me that when you feel bad about yourself, you allow anything to happen to you.

CHAPTER 22

I sat down with the manager of the bar and told her I was quitting. "I can't be here anymore."

Besides, fall was just around the corner and I never intended to work through the school year. This helped reassure my mind I wasn't quitting because I felt threatened by Reed. That was more power than I was willing to relinquish.

But still, I scurried home like prey, out of breath and darting through crowds. Now he'd even stolen daylight.

My relationship with Reed wasn't something my parents and I discussed often, but after Reed was arrested, things were different and there was no point in pretending.

"Get a copy of the security footage," my mom told me over the phone. "We should have it in case we need to send it to our lawyer."

My stomach tightened with the mention of a lawyer. This was getting too big.

They were mature eyes on a situation I didn't yet understand. A situation that, for some reason, felt juvenile and humiliating. The bar emailed me fifteen seconds of security footage, and back then, I watched it only once. (Now, years later, I've seen the video countless times. Reed walking, pushing one ear of his headphones off, his lips pressing into mine, his hands gripping my waist and head, my back arching. Interestingly, Reed isn't the man in the video I'm most angry at. No. It's the man in the white button up who is approaching the front door when he sees Reed grab me. The man whose gaze lingers on us, just for a second, and walks back upstairs to join his friends on the rooftop bar.)

"Your dad and I were talking," my mom continued. "We want to fly you out here, that way you'll be out of the city. A distraction for you, and this way we know you're safe. What do you think?"

My parents were on vacation in South Carolina on a road trip, just the two of them.

The next day, I stood on the sidewalk with a small suitcase and hailed a cab. I pressed play on "Leaving on a Jet Plane" and, with vacant eyes, watched Toronto fly by the window. The city where I'd grown up was starting to feel tainted, an itch to leave it forever growing stronger.

The moment I sat down on board the flight, my seatmate, who had been on a call, put his phone down and gleefully said to me, "Do you see who's beside you?" His eyes bursting with boyish excitement.

I turned to my left. Directly across the aisle sat Bill Cosby.

"Oh, no way." Apparently, I'd entered an alternate universe.

As the plane rattled down the runway and lifted off high above Toronto, I gripped the armrests. I've always hated flying. The flight attendant was sitting directly in front of me, facing my direction. "It's okay," she mouthed, with a warm smile.

With each foot we climbed, Reed's apartment shrank. My eyes were puffy and heavy, and my body hummed like there'd been a death.

Throughout the flight, a handful of giddy passengers formed a line down the aisle to meet Cosby. I sat with my headphones in, reducing their small talk to muffles, occasionally glancing over at their excitement. Once the line had cleared, I noticed the flight attendant gesturing toward me, so I popped my headphones out.

"Sorry?" I asked her.

"Do you want a photo with Mr. Cosby? I saw you looking over!" She asked me with a huge, expectant smile.

I turned slightly toward him. "No, no. That's alright. I don't want to bother him, but thank you." I nodded in his direction and went to put my headphones back in.

"Are you sure? He flies with us often, and he really doesn't mind!" Maybe she thought it would cheer up the girl who looked like she hadn't slept in weeks, was obviously terrified of planes, and was keeping one eye on the ogling passengers.

I turned toward Bill Cosby, about to politely attempt to decline for a second time, but instead, he waved me over.

Reluctantly, I unclipped my seatbelt. Feeling the stares of every passenger, I handed my cell phone to the flight attendant and knelt next to Bill Cosby. He shook my hand.

"What's your name?" He asked.

"It's Callie. Nice to meet you." I squeezed out a response.

"And why are you heading south?"

"Oh, um, my parents are down there. Just meeting them for a short vacation."

As he peppered me with small talk, his warm, beefy hand held my small clammy one. I felt my arm muscles twitch every few seconds, searching for the mutual decision to release, which eventually came.

We smiled for a photo.

"You can't be nervous when Bill Cosby is on your flight, now can you!" The flight attendant beamed. I smiled half-heartedly.

"You're nervous?" Cosby asked me as I climbed back into my own seat.

"Yes, I hate flying." I glanced down at the surreal photo now living on my cell phone and said, "Thank you." I put my headphones back in and tried to zone out for the remainder of the flight.

As soon as we arrived at the gate, I unclipped my seatbelt once again, gathered my things, and waited eagerly in the aisle to be let off the plane. As we stood waiting for the doors to open, Cosby stood closely behind me. I glanced back at the rest of the passengers, their eyes still glued to the superstar in our midst, everyone quiet.

"So, do you not fly often?" I heard him say.

I looked around. Was he talking to me? Apparently, yes. "Oh, um, I actually do fly pretty often," I said, a bit shocked he was striking up another conversation.

"So, what's it going to take then?" He jokingly barked.

". . . What's what going to take?" I smiled nervously.

"What's it going to take for you not to be scared?"

"Oh . . . You know, I have no idea," I said, willing the doors to open. Then they did. I shot him a polite smile, threw my headphones back on one last time, and power walked my way off the flight. Warm southern air seeped through the airport walls. I had no idea what South Carolina was even like, but there I was, two days after my ex-boyfriend was arrested, justifying my fear of flying to Bill Cosby.

When I saw my parents, I mouthed to them with big, wide eyes and pointed subtly, "Look." Behind me, Bill Cosby was shuffling his feet, which I remember as being in slippers. Can that be right?

That afternoon, my parents and I sat at a seaside restaurant watching palm trees sway. Salty air transported me, took me away, allowed me to pretend.

The miles between me and Reed lent me the courage to ask my parents, "I got the security footage from the bar. Do you want to see it?" I asked them, holding up my cell phone as if it was some shiny treasure I'd just pulled from the ground.

My mom shook her head violently, "I don't want to see it, no."

"Yeah. Okay." How dumb of me to ask, of course no one wanted to see it.

It would be a few years before Cosby's horrific behaviour reached the top of the headlines, years before #MeToo, and before I personally became aware of his long history of sexually assaulting and raping numerous women, with more than sixty women coming forward.

Having learned about these accusations only after our airplane meeting, I felt sick at the memory of this interaction and its horrific, menacing timing in my life. He was, and is, a true monster among us. So strange that he appeared next to me that day, as I was escaping my very own monster. But it was a haunting reminder that predators come in all shapes, sizes, and statuses. They can be the quiet boy a few doors down or America's most treasured dad, making millions of people laugh and, devastatingly, feel safe.

But how are we ever to feel safe, truly safe, when abusers can be anything? Twenty-five-year-old neighbours and beloved actors.

Years later, my mom and I talked about those South Carolina days. She said, "I waited for you to bring it up and talk about it, but you didn't. You seemed so calm and pleasant, happy, even. We handled it all wrong. We should have asked more questions and talked it through, but we thought you wanted a distraction. Or maybe you weren't ready to talk about it. We should have asked. I still think about that and the mistakes we made."

Instead of talking, we sipped sweet tea, walked along the sand, and I buried my head in it.

Although we wouldn't realize it for years, this short trip set a long precedent. My parents believed I didn't want to share, and I believed it was my burden to carry, alone. The established silence dried like concrete, and I never found it in myself to break through.

I don't know how I feel about anything.
There is a block in my mind that doesn't
allow me to feel anything Reed did to me.
PTSD? Maybe. No way I walked away
without being scarred by the things he
did to me.
I'm not healed and nothing is <u>ok</u>.

CHAPTER 23

In the weeks after Reed's arrest, I drifted through the city as if it had been bombed, and I was left alone to survey the smoky damage. The restaurants where we'd eaten, the parks where we'd sat, the sidewalks where we'd held hands, they were grey. I wandered with dead eyes, searching for ways to fill my time and distract my brain from the memories. My stomach ached for the sticky summer in his small blue bedroom, his hands touching my face. The city lured me back in with memories of when he loved me. I was battling a true addiction.

While in South Carolina, I'd received a call from Detective Liu. In the backseat of my parents' car, I hugged my knees, and he explained Reed was out on bail. He was now under strict conditions; he was not to contact me either directly or indirectly, he could not be within two hundred metres of any place I may be (the bar where I worked, my school campus, etc.), and a few other conditions. A court date was scheduled for a few weeks later where he could plead guilty, take a peace bond or he could choose to take the charges to trial and fight them.

It was done. I'd left him.

Unbeknownst to me, it was at this point that, statistically, I was most likely to die.

Loud are the what-ifs.

Knowing these rules were placed on us by something stronger than our addiction left me with wide eyes, scanning every room and sidewalk for his dark hair. I saw him only twice. The first time, we were walking on opposite sides of the street. I caught just a glimpse, but I could spot that walk anywhere, barely lifting his knees. The second time was at a bar. I was playing pool with Blake and Logan. The bar had a small but famous concert venue at the back, and when the show ended, Reed stepped out and walked right by us, heading for the door. Logan followed, making sure he left. I don't think he saw me.

I hated that people in my life now saw him as the enemy. It was only out of an abundance of care and a desire to make me feel safe, but I didn't see Reed that way, even when I pretended to.

It took a long time for my body to begin to relax and disengage. I flinched if someone passed by me too closely on the sidewalk. My nerves jumped with every car horn or crash of construction. I made sure the street-level door to my condo building locked behind me and contemplated removing my name from the intercom. Anxiety swallowed me whole if a man paid me any sort of attention, worried they weren't what they seemed, that they would humiliate me or lure me into making all the wrong decisions — again. Men brought only fear. One day, a security guard at the bar where I used to work texted me just to check in. *Hey, just wanted to make sure you were doing okay. Let me know if I can do anything.* I panicked and blocked his number without replying.

The police kept me in the loop about Reed post-arrest: an occasional call from the detective or a letter in the mail. As far as I know, Reed never did any jail time. I wish I'd paid closer attention — to everything. And while I do have some records, I wish I'd collected all of them, saved all the letters, and asked much more detailed questions in the name of self-protection (something I did eventually end up doing, but still, there are gaps in information). At such a young age, I'd had enough. I didn't want to know what was happening with Reed anymore — my life had been consumed by him for too long — I'd reached my limit. I didn't want to know who bailed him out. I didn't want to know he was free to meet his next girlfriend. Now it was my turn to pretend these things didn't matter.

Over time, the updates ended. I moved and forgot to update the police with my new address, which put an end to the letters. I stopped using the email address I gave the police because it was the one Reed had, too. I let Reed and all his complications drift away, and instead of it being the loudest voice inside my head, I let it become background noise. I hoped it would become inaudible, but that didn't happen. At a certain point, it plateaued at a permanent hum.

The drama had cooled, and I was alone. Like disappearing ripples, check-ins became less frequent, the shock wore off, and now, I was just a girl who'd broken up with her boyfriend. Common. Normal. A girl going through a breakup. It was a simplicity that, up until these deadened moments to myself, I felt hadn't really been allowed. But stripped of its sirens and fireworks, this was still just a breakup.

And like any other breakup, I missed the person who had become my best friend. I was lonely for him, wanting to pick up the phone and call, having to break habits and extinguish any hope of hearing his voice, wondering what he was up to. I slept in his T-shirts and listened to his favourite songs, anything to keep him close in quiet ways no one but me could hear.

Grappling with the immense loss seemed forbidden.

I knew leaving him was what was best. But I also wondered if we would obey these new rules. It wouldn't be the first time we snuck around, and we knew how to do it well. Lies came easy, and I'd learned to live with the betrayal that followed me to his apartment. I'd been living under his reign for so long, I no longer knew how to walk free.

Me and Stephen's brief relationship ended around Halloween when he told me after a dinner date, "I don't think we should see each other anymore. I don't want to be in a relationship, and I'm worried I'm leading you on." I understood why he thought I might be feeling that way considering we texted about our days and carved pumpkins in his living room. But being someone's girlfriend — someone who wasn't Reed — was never on the table. Not at that point. I wanted Stephen's comfort, but not as a boyfriend. Nothing could possibly have been more threatening.

And yet, his words ripped the stitches wide open, which I couldn't understand.

I was too raw to be trusted with anyone's feelings, too debilitated to properly identify any emotions. Stephen did what was right by both of us.

You were never a safe place for me. I just kept hoping that would change.

CHAPTER 24

Escaping my abusive boyfriend handed me an overwhelming appreciation for regular, mundane life. It meant a second chance at my twenties and an intoxicating sense of freedom, only comparable to the first time driving without a parent in the passenger seat. Spending time with Marley, honestly answering questions about my love life, flirting with boys at school — everything glistened just a little brighter.

One year after Reed's arrest, I landed an internship at the audio production company my dad had founded (and sold a few years prior). Working at his company had been a dream of mine ever since I was a little kid sitting with him at the kitchen table over breakfast whining, "You're *so* lucky you get to go to work and do whatever you want. I have to go to school." He laughed and said, "I wouldn't say I get to do whatever I want. You just wait, you'll miss school when you're working!" But I knew he loved his job, how could he not? His office had four recording studios, guitars hanging on the walls, fish tanks, multi-coloured iMacs on each desk, and rows of candy jars.

I was eager to prove I deserved my place at the company, even as an intern, and although I'd been wandering around that office for as long as I could remember, walking through the glass doors as an intern was entirely new. No longer was I scooping candy into bowls to bring back to my dad's office and devour on the couch while he talked music briefs. Now, my place was in the casting department running Pro Tools, a recording software. For each role in either a radio or television voiceover commercial, around twenty actors would come in to audition. I brought the actors into the studio, adjusted their mic, and headed back into the studio to hit record. Next to me sat the director who told the actors what the client was looking for and gave them direction after each take. I kept my eyes and ears open, making mental notes of how each director spoke to the actors, how they approached the seasoned ones, how they delivered feedback when the takes weren't working, how they guided each performance.

Outside of the casting department, directors were at the top of the food chain. Their roles at the company were not only to direct the actors but to run the entire recording session. Once actors were chosen from the casting, a final recording session was booked. In came the advertising agency (like BBDO Canada, Publicis Groupe, Cossette, Leo Burnett Toronto) and the client (like TD Bank, Bell Canada, Ford Motor Company, IKEA). The director ran the whole day — made sure the session ran on time, wrangled the actors, took the feedback from the agency as well as the client, instructed the sound engineer — all while making sure morale and energy stayed high. After all, studio days are fun days for the agency and client.

On top of directing the voiceover, overseeing music, and sound effects, they were also the ones to bring in the business.

I knew before even stepping foot into the casting studio that I wanted to be a director — a full director — like my dad. I poured everything I had into the internship, doing my best to be brave and ask for opportunity. I wanted to learn and show how eager I was but, at the same time, make it clear I knew my place. I was trying to be a good intern, not the founder's kid (while acknowledging I am in fact a nepo baby).

Before the internship ended that August, I was called into the boss's office.

"It's clear you fit right in here, and you've been great over the summer," he told me. I'd heard his name around my house since I was a little kid. "We'd love to offer you a full-time job in the casting department."

My eyes practically popped out of my head. "Really?"

"Yes, and we know you aren't finished school, so we can make adjustments if you want to finish and graduate."

I knew immediately what I wanted to do, and that was to leave school, start working, and leave my old life behind.

As a full-time employee, I was even more determined and — looking back — perhaps embarrassingly gutsy and naive. After my first year, I asked for a meeting with the boss and told him, "I want to be a director." I asked if I could occasionally sit with him while he did his job — listened to castings, took calls with the agency, briefed the music writers — so I could learn. Soon, I was carving out time once a week to sit in the studio, watching commercials for every major brand be recorded with the biggest ad agencies in the world. And not too long after that, I was promoted to director. I was by far the youngest director at the company — and in the country. The other directors were the partners, and all men.

Those two years changed every beat of my life. While my friends were finishing their degrees, I was working nine-to-five, sitting in sales meetings, and meeting with creative directors.

It was that job, that company, that gave me an opportunity to reinvent myself, to meet myself as an adult, to pull away from painful routines. Although most people around me outside of the industry didn't know it, my role was big, especially for my age. I directed a Coca-Cola commercial with licensed music by the Ramones, I directed many Tim Hortons commercials, as well as New Balance, Volkswagen, Tylenol, and many more. I went into agency boardrooms to give presentations, and I travelled to the South of France for the Cannes Lions Awards for advertising where we lined up client lunches and dinners.

My life exploded beyond Reed, and it was unrecognizable. Earning career accomplishments shrank his memory inside of me every single day. For the first time in years, I was able to feel proud of myself and others felt proud of me, too. No longer was I lost and floundering, self-harming and wasting days with sadness. Somehow, I was actually ahead. A certain confidence began to awaken inside of me — a spark I hadn't felt since high school. Since before Reed.

My mind rarely thought of him or the insecure version of myself he'd constructed. Finally, I felt the way I imagined I would as an adult. I believed I'd moved on, closed the chapter, and escaped unscathed. There was nowhere I wanted to be less than back in his bedroom, hating myself.

Don't reopen those scars.

CHAPTER 25

My eyes opened and I felt my lungs involuntarily gasp for the relief of air. I sat up, propping myself onto one elbow, and lay still for a few seconds, allowing my body to remember where it was in its own time.

Through morning eyes, my apartment was blurry. The light was sneaking through the blinds. I let my elbow release and fell back down onto my pillows. I put my hand down the front of my distressed Harley davidson T-shirt, then the back. I felt my arms and my neck. Every inch of my skin was cold and wet. My heart still racing.

Seconds earlier, I was running down hallways, through empty trains, and over dark sidewalks. I was screaming for help as the gap between Reed and I shrank. I yelled for two strangers on the train, a desperate scream, yelling that the person chasing me was dangerous, that he was going to hurt me. I was pleading for their help. But they turned away and dissolved into thin air, like two ghosts, leaving just Reed and me, alone in our shared experience.

To leave that world, all I had to do was open my eyes. I gave my body time to remember we were miles away from that life, from Reed. Two years had passed since I ran from him through the hallway of his Toronto apartment building.

My chest dripped with sweat.

After a few minutes, I peeled myself out of bed and stuck my hand between the blinds of my bedroom windows. There were no more shadows. I was far away from my previous life — a feeling which helped to lower my heart rate.

I made my way to the shower, hoping a burst of water would help bring me back into reality. As I washed my hair, I replayed the dream; Reed doing his best to push through my apartment door, me pushing back with all my strength. Water trickled down my back.

With my head resting on the tiled wall, I realized, with great relief, how scared I had just been. Fear. What a relief. Fear was clear. Fear made sense. Fear confirmed everything I believed I felt next to Reed in the end. Things got cloudy when my dreams filled me with nostalgia and warmth for him. But this — pure anxiety — wasn't cloaked in anything else, and for that, I was grateful. I stepped out of the shower and shifted my focus to coffee.

But a cloud hovered over me for the rest of the day. The vividness of the dream wouldn't leave me alone, wouldn't lift, as others had. Although my days were now spent on a different planet surrounded by people with no knowledge of my history, my nights were infiltrated by Reed and his dark eyes. In my sleep, he hunted me.

I opened my phone and found Marley's name. *I had a vivid dream about Reed last night.* Staring at my phone, my thumb refused to press send. I needed an outlet, but Marley wasn't the answer. At this point, she had listened to me talk through my relationship with Reed for years. How much was I willing to unload onto her? I slowly deleted the text and felt the weight of the dream re-enter my body.

I'm probably going to carry you around for a very long time.

CHAPTER 26

THE ARTIST

Toronto stood still with traffic. Sweat trickled down my back as I waited for the streetcar. I'd dressed too warm for early October. A good friend of mine was having a birthday dinner at a restaurant across town in Liberty Village, and as badly as I didn't feel like making the journey, I knew I would regret missing it.

The group was seated at a large table right in the middle of the restaurant. My friend, the birthday girl, sat at the head of the table.

"Hi!" I rushed over and hugged her. "So sorry I'm late, the streetcar took forever. Happy birthday!"

"That's okay! I know, it's brutal. Come, come! Have a seat!" She turned to face the rest of the table and gestured toward the only empty seat at the other end. "Do you know anyone over there?"

"Hm. Not sure but don't worry about me!"

I sat down in the empty seat. Next to me was a blonde guy I felt I recognized.

"Oh, hey!" He said as I got comfortable.

"Hi! I'm Callie," I reached out to shake his hand. "Nice to meet you."

"I'm James. Nice to meet you, too." James was smiley and warm.

As the evening went on, we got to chatting. He was incredibly charismatic and outgoing. Something about him was definitely familiar.

Narrowing my eyes, I asked, "Were you in graphic design?"

"I was. Were you?" He smiled back at me.

"I thought I recognized you," I said to him, my own smile growing.

"Yeah? Did we have a class together?" He turned his whole body to face mine.

"I think so, yeah." I pretended I wasn't sure. I was. "I feel like you never stayed for the whole thing. Am I right?"

"That does sound right," he laughed.

In class, he was tough to miss. Cool, good looking, and always sitting at the back. I'd noticed him — a few times.

Across the table from us was a girl clearly interested in James as well. She had amazing dark curly hair and a big smile. She was beautiful and much more fun than me. Several times throughout dinner, she made her way around the table and sat on James's lap. They'd clearly had a thing, past or present.

"What are you doing after this?" She slung a long arm around James's shoulders.

I'd made myself a vow, months before, that I would never again let anyone, especially a man, dictate how I felt about myself. Never again was I going to let my world revolve around a guy. Never was I going to compete. I wasn't interested in fighting for this guy's attention, and any willingness to care had evaporated long before.

I smiled and turned to the girl on my other side.

At the end of the meal, the group was going back to my friend's apartment for a couple drinks before heading out to another bar. Something was percolating inside of me, and I knew the feeling all too well. Over dinner, James had won me over a little bit, and now, my stomach was telling me to run. Run. Far away and fast. This wasn't a game I was interested in playing.

James took a couple steps toward the door before turning around and flashing yet another smile. "Callie! You're coming to the bar, right?" His teeth were straight and his blonde hair swooped like a Disney prince.

I was tempted.

"No, I have plans with a friend but have fun." I lied. Kind of.

"You should coooome," James said sweetly.

I'd lost my will to play any dating games — something that was once the most fun part of my young life. I felt like I'd just been through a war. Any excitement I had to date, to play the part, to get my hopes up, to dress up, had all dried up. Instead, I went to Blake's apartment to watch *Friends*.

"How was the birthday dinner?" Blake asked, as she handed me a glass of Malbec.

"I think I met someone I kind of like," I said as we snuggled in under a blanket.

"You did? Who?"

"This guy, James. He was nice. He wanted me to go to the bar but . . . I didn't want to go." I was defeated at just the thought.

"Ooo! Well, just message him." Her raspy voice commanded.

"Nah."

It turns out this was just the beginning of my and James's little chapter. He reached out to me shortly after and not much longer after that we started hanging out. We ended up casually seeing each other for a while, on and off, with no expectations, and never had a conversation about where it was going or what it "was."

One weekend, James and I went to his parents' cottage in Muskoka, just the two of us. I woke up late the first morning and threw on a sweater. Tiptoeing down the stairs, the sun was streaming through the cottage's big front windows overlooking the still lake. It was late fall. The house was quiet, and James was nowhere to be found. Then I heard the hum of a machine coming from outside.

Stepping out into the sunny day, I found James shirtless, carving a totem pole with a chainsaw twenty feet in the air. For real. Wearing just shorts, work boots, and goggles, he stood on a makeshift plank carving beautiful details into a tree trunk high above the ground.

He saw me and turned off the chainsaw.

"Wow, that's amazing!" I yelled up to him.

"You think so?" He smiled proudly.

"Yeah! It's really beautiful. Just casually carving with a chainsaw, huh?"

"You know!" He took his goggles off. "What are you gonna do today?"

"I don't know. Read, maybe?" I looked around. Leaves were falling, and the lake was calm.

"Nice cottage outfit you got there," he gestured toward me with a coy smile. Blake had lent me her knee-high Docs. "Want me to come in and light a fire for you?"

That weekend, we went for a chilly boat ride, watched movies, made dinner, and talked by the fire. At no point did I wonder if this meant I was his girlfriend or if that's where it was headed. I didn't have the desire for anything that would have come with a full-fledged relationship. This was all I could handle. If I had a boyfriend, he'd expect an invitation to my parents' place or to hang out with me at Blake's. That was too close. This, with James, was perfect.

One night as we lay on my bed, legs intertwined, I tried to open up about what I'd been through with Reed. Although we mostly kept each other at arm's length, something inside of me wanted him to know, offering him the opportunity to undo the things that had been done.

I hated that I felt that way.

"I know I've hinted at this, but my last relationship was a pretty bad situation. I think it may have messed me up a bit." I treaded lightly, unsure of how much I really wanted to divulge or how to word something so big in a casual way.

With a shrug, he said, "Well, we all have our baggage."

My stomach tightened, and I stared at the ceiling. I missed Reed and the way he made me feel so full, like I'd never need anything else. Now I was left wanting.

James's response, or lack thereof, was a good reminder that while we optically seemed intimate and close, just beneath the surface, there was a vast emptiness. I let it go but felt myself detach just a little bit more. A less exhausted version of myself would have pressed about how he could possibly say something so flippant about an experience that weighed so heavily on me when I was clearly trying to open up and talk about it. But again, I didn't have the energy. James was a good person, and with hindsight and time to heal, I see he was most likely trying to downplay it for my benefit. To make me feel like it was okay, that I wasn't somehow "damaged" or "broken" beyond his desire.

THE MAGNET

James and I stopped seeing each other after I met Brett. Brett was a friend of a friend who I'd always had my eye on, as did a lot of people, but I never thought anything would come of it. It was clear that he and I were very different people. He was the life-of-the-party guy. Quite literally, all he wanted to do was party. Brett meant fun. He had the loudest voice in the room and a wildly contagious laugh. I think that's what attracted me most; he was the antithesis of Reed. Brett was like sunshine; the kind of guy who spent his weekends on Lake Joseph with "the boys," was rarely without a backwards baseball cap, loved country music, and never missed a Leafs game. He was also really cute. Green eyes and thick dark hair with sprinkles of grey.

Brett and I started dating after finding ourselves out with friends and both single. At one point during the night, he turned to me with a devastatingly cute smile and said, "I like you. You're trouble."

It carried on for about six months. At first, Brett and I also had no rules or expectations. I felt more strongly for him than I had for anyone since Reed. But still, I was nowhere near ready to be in a relationship, which would ultimately mean bringing him into my life in real ways.

One day, Brett and I were out for sushi when I got a text from Marley. The message caught my attention right away. *I just saw something. I wasn't sure if I should tell you but decided it's best for you to know.* I stared at my phone waiting for the next message to come through. Then I saw the very thing I feared: a picture of Reed and his new girlfriend. Worst of all, it was a girl Marley and I recognized. She was a bartender at the corner bar.

Brett put down his chopsticks and stared at me with sweet, concerned eyes from across the small table. "What's going on?"

After a long silence, eventually I choked out the words, "Marley just sent me a picture of Reed and his new girlfriend. I kind of know her."

"Oh man. I'm sorry, that's rough." After a long pause with no response, he said, "Are you okay?"

"Yeah. I guess so. I just hate that his life has moved on with no issues. He just . . . moved on. Got a new girlfriend. No problem." I couldn't take my eyes off the picture. "It isn't fair that he just . . ."

Brett stared back at me with soft worry. "I'm sorry."

I felt my eyes start to sting. Not only because I was jealous, because I was, but also because it didn't make sense. He found a girl willing to date him? Didn't she know what he was like?

Didn't she know he'd been arrested for assaulting me? Didn't he love me anymore?

How pathetic.

I knew her, just a little bit, but I did know her. She was beautiful. I always thought she looked like Emma Watson, and in the very few interactions we had, she was kind and cool. She seemed quiet and a little bit shy, reserved and often alone, but clearly by choice. And now she was with him. She was pretty, blonde, cool, docile, just like Reed. He must have already forgotten me.

Knowing her and I were friends on Facebook, without any concern for Brett or the meal we were eating, I opened my Facebook app and searched her name. But it turned up no results. I tried different spellings. Same with Instagram. She didn't exist to me anymore. This made my stomach turn. Who knows what Reed had told her about me and how "crazy" he'd made me out to be, just as he'd painted his ex out to be before me, but whatever he said was enough for her to block me on all platforms.

I wanted to be the only one whose life he ripped apart, and I wasn't sure why I felt that way.

One thing I did know for sure, and instantly: she and I were connected and always would be. To this day, I often think of her.

Brett and I eventually decided to make a go of it as boyfriend and girlfriend. It progressed to the point where I didn't like the idea of anyone else getting his attention.

For reasons I had trouble articulating but understood perfectly, having a boyfriend paralyzed me with fear, like treading dark waters. I was frequently visited by my old friends guilt and shame. Throughout our relationship, I fought every day to remind myself it was okay to have a boyfriend, normal, even. I'd grown accustomed to crushing guilt when I was with Reed, so used to lying and knowing what I was doing was wrong, that spending time with Brett brought the exact same guilt purely out of habit. I tried to remind myself Brett and I had mutual friends. If he had a violent side, if he was dangerous, I'd know. He was safe. We knew him, and above all else, he was a kind person, though sometimes not boyfriend material.

Part of me was terrified of him.

Brett and I really tried, and we had a lot of fun together. So much fun that I occasionally showed up to work hungover and having not slept. We saw movies, binged *Band of Brothers* in bed, ordered sushi, walked Dex, sat at his regular bar in a dark corner booth drinking vodka sodas and cheap beer. We did a lot. It was a nice change of pace from my last relationship, where we rarely saw the light of day, and he didn't know my friends. He also unofficially moved in — I'd leave him for work at the studio in the morning, and when I came home, he was still there, hanging with my sister.

Brett was a buoyant person, but throughout our time together, I learned there was a lot more going on beneath his happy-go-lucky exterior. He wasn't just the effervescent disco ball we all watched. Instead, he was a complex person with doubts, worries, self-esteem struggles, trying to find his place. He was much more layered than I originally gave him credit for, and that was nice. Brett also showed great interest and care in understanding that clearly something heavy had happened with Reed. One night, I shared a few details about the confusing sexual experiences I'd had. Brett carried no judgment while we lay on our stomachs and watched the security footage from the bar. Brett was the first person I talked to about that day, and to his credit, he made it a safe place to do so. I wasn't sad while we talked. I wasn't anxious. I felt it nowhere in my body. Oddly, sharing with Brett left me slightly smug and confident. In that moment, I didn't fear anyone or anything. I was silently reminding Brett that I was the experienced one here, and he wasn't about to hurt me. Nothing he could do would shock or impress me. Emotionally, I was untouchable.

While we were together, I was hit with a bad flu. Brett stayed up with me all night. He ran to the twenty-four-hour drug store to get me more supplies and rubbed my back while I coughed until I gagged. When steam was my only relief, he waited outside the bathroom door while I stood in the shower. He wanted to be a good boyfriend, but throughout our relationship, I was keeping him at arm's length and as his girlfriend, it was unfair. I dangled it but never told him I loved him and would occasionally turn cold for no reason. During arguments, he expressed how hurt he was that I didn't seem to love him the way he loved me, and I just stared back at him, stone-faced, unable to provide any reassurance at all. My guard was so far up, I couldn't get emotional with him about anything. I couldn't seem to push myself any further, no matter how hard I tried. I was dead inside.

"You're the only girlfriend in the world who can see their boyfriend this hurt and feel nothing," he told me, one night after an argument about me being aloof. He was right. I wouldn't let him love me.

I searched for a kind way to say that most of the time, I felt nothing. For anyone.

Eventually, Brett broke up with me, and I deserved it. I wasn't in love with him, and he knew it. I'm not sure he really loved me either — I think I was indifferent, so he craved my attention. Somehow, I'd become Reed.

I wasn't healthy enough to be trusted with anyone's feelings. The memory of Brett fills me with unease and shame, and comfort and warmth. I should have ended our relationship. Instead, I dragged him through the mud of my healing, and iced him out whenever I lacked the capacity. But I liked how I felt around him. Brett made the world a little bit brighter, a reminder of nice men. Gentle men. Men who aren't clouds of darkness. There are people who want to have fun and make sure I have fun, too. There are boyfriends who will rub my back all night while I cough.

The day we broke up, I called Marley from a rainy dog walk.

She told me, "I really think you need to talk to someone about everything that happened with Reed. I know you think you got out *unscathed*. You've said it many times. But there's just no way that's true, and you can't expect to let someone new in until you've worked through it."

Standing in the pouring rain, I said, "I'll think about it. But I think I'm fine."

It was, in fact, good old-fashioned avoidance.

I wish someone would steal this journal and read it so they would know how my brain works without me having to explain it.

CHAPTER 27

Memories began to awaken from hibernation. Heavy with guilt, I knew I needed to talk about it and that was inevitably going to fall upon the very people who had already spent hours listening. For this reason, it took months before I told anyone these memories were showing up in my back seat, behind me in the mirror, beside me in the shower. Before I started talking, tears filled my ears at night. I began journaling again, painting again, searching for an outlet that didn't involve subjecting my friends to more of my problems. I searched for outlets that wouldn't destroy my life when a snide little voice in my head told me to start drinking. Really, really drinking.

Band-aid solutions — like crying myself to sleep — worked for a short time. But things started to snowball, and my lens turned familiarly bleak. My inner arms were burning, calling out for the same punishment I'd inflicted regularly three years before. I felt darker tendencies swirling around in my stomach, itching to get out and cause a bit of destruction.

As I learned through my own experience, the brain will make a lot of choices for us about how we carry our trauma. My brain closed the file tightly and did not open it again until a few years had passed, and still, it wasn't fully open. My mind chose to forget certain things entirely until I was reminded by a moment in a TV show or movie (cut to me sobbing in the movie theatre during *I, Tonya*). It wasn't that I was actively thinking about it, but I was unable to put it into words — I rarely, if ever, directly thought about the things that happened, not the violence anyway. For a while, my mind never let me go there in much detail. It was easier that way.

I did, however, innately understand the importance of sharing painful thoughts that swirl around my mind like a tornado uprooting every memory, mistake, loss, and stress I've ever experienced. I learned this as a teenager when my mental health was at its lowest point thanks to crushing panic attacks. I didn't really have a choice; if I didn't scream for help, I wasn't able to get through my day. So I shared. I talked. I tried to explain to my parents what it felt like to be pacing, hitting my chest over and over again with a deep sense of impending doom. I tried to explain how my heart would race, and I felt like I could run a marathon but also like I might pass out while my lips, fingers, and toes tingled, my stomach flipped, and I took deep breaths to keep from vomiting, all while fighting off thoughts of a welcomed death. I tried to explain these things because it was too heavy to carry on my own. It wasn't easy to describe, but I tried all the time. It got me used to sharing. I learned how to feel comforted even when the eyes looking back at me were unsure and unable to relate. But they were trying and I was trying and that's what's important. I packed these skills tightly into my back pocket, ready to pull them out no matter where I was or who I was with: family, friends, colleagues, strangers. Learning these skills was purely about survival.

I was very open about aspects of my struggle with mental health, even at work. I made it clear to the studio partners I needed to go to therapy once a week for an hour. I asked to sit in the front seat of the cab on our way to presentations so I wouldn't panic from claustrophobia in the back. I did what I had to in order to help myself succeed while trudging through panic so intense it's indescribable.

But when it came to Reed, I struggled. Back to square one, I didn't feel capable of opening up. I didn't have the language beyond the very basics, which never covered such intricate nuance. Maybe I just lacked the desire to revisit it. But often those who have experienced trauma have to go through the process of sharing — however that looks — of making sense of something and accepting it, before moving forward in a healthy way.

It's like that one box of clothes we should just get rid of, but instead, we throw it under our bed, convinced that means we'll never have to deal with it again. Then you turn around and it's moving day. Once again, you're face to face with that box. No matter what, it's going to be there with you — apartment to apartment, house to house — until you deal with it.

The moment I felt ready to dip my toe in wasn't spurred on by anything in particular. It's so personal, but in my experience, there will be a moment — just as there was a moment I knew I had to end my relationship with Reed — that I felt ready to talk, just a little.

So, I told a couple of my best friends what was going on, beginning with the thought that was haunting me most: my body still feeling like Reed's property, thanks to the things I knew he could look at any time he wanted.

One evening, I invited myself over to my good friend Cat's. I lay in the fetal position under the covers, searching for words to do the pain justice. "I'm really struggling with the Reed stuff. And there's something in particular. One specific thing that I just can't . . ."

What started as a calm conversation quickly turned into me sobbing and shaking, curled up in a ball, while she rubbed my back.

"You can tell me. There is no judgment here. You can tell me. You'll feel better." Cat assured me.

I sat up, eyes puffy, chest aching. Warm tears dripped along my chin. "He . . . He probably still has a video of us having sex and some photos that I found on his laptop."

"Okay, that's okay. That's a pretty common thing to do. What are you worried about exactly? Can you pinpoint it?"

I took a deep breath and tried to think — really think — what I was worried about exactly. It's not like I'm famous. Why did this upset me so much?

I told her, "I think I hate my body now. It doesn't feel like it's *mine*. It can't be mine when someone so awful and dangerous and scary also owns it. And truly, I'm scared that if it ever came out, I would be humiliated. What if it ruins my career somehow?"

Cat and I talked for a couple of hours, and I shared only vague details. She assured me that no matter what, my life wouldn't fall apart, and I had nothing to be ashamed of.

"So many people do that! Plus, if it was ever shared, it would reflect badly on him, not you. This isn't twenty years ago." I felt myself sink into her bed, happy to lose myself ever so slightly in someone else's world, momentarily escaping my own. Once again, my life was suffocating me.

As I opened the door to my apartment later that night, I felt like a fraud. I knew I'd left my own world in order to truthfully let my feelings out, to release some of the things that were bothering me. As I stepped back into my life once again, dread filled my stomach. The release hadn't actually released me at all. I couldn't find the source of the bleeding.

Over the following weeks, as I began talking about the abuse with my friends, I was floored by their reactions. Laine and I sat at a chic downtown bar one night, surrounded by overpriced drinks and loud music, and I shared a bit about what was eating me from the inside.

"He was abusive during the relationship. He threw me against the wall, pinned me to the bed, things like that. Have I told you that before?" I said, studying Laine's eyes for a reaction.

Laine, one of my closest friends who saw me frequently while Reed and I were together said, "You've never told me any of this."

"What?" I set my drink down on the white marble bar. "Yes, of course I have."

"Callie! No. I didn't know any of this," she told me, brows furrowing.

"You didn't know he was violent with me?"

"No. I had no idea. I thought he was depressed and maybe it was taking a toll on your mental health, too. I thought he was a difficult person to deal with and it was starting to really weigh on you. Anyone could see that. But I never knew there was abuse or I would have said something. I would have taken you away." My insides warmed up, just a little bit.

I asked a couple of other close friends, including Claire, my best friend since I was fourteen, who now lived in New York. She had a similar response. "All I know is he showed up at your work and grabbed you or something like that? I remember you telling me that story," she said one night as I walked Dex around the city, talking to her on the phone.

"But I never told you anything else?" I was trying to piece my own life together.

"Well, when you told me what happened at work that day, I said something like, 'That is so unexpected.' And you said, 'It isn't *that* unexpected.'" Claire told me.

Then I asked my therapist who I'd been seeing since I was eighteen.

"No," she said. "You never told me there was physical abuse."

That one was the most shocking revelation of all. I was certain I'd told her intimate details of the abuse both as it was happening and in the few years since.

". . . No way. Did you suspect it?" I asked her, confused by my own actions.

"I suspected there was something going on, yes. I believed there was emotional abuse happening. I knew he disappeared a lot, and I knew that was incredibly difficult for you. But you never told me about any physical abuse, no."

I turned my attention out the window of her twentieth-floor office. Normally, seeing people in their little cubicles going about their days downtown made my problems feel instantly small, the scope of the city shrinking my worries. I imagined they were dealing with stressful emails, deals worth millions of dollars, and angry bosses. But that day, it made no difference.

The one thing my therapist did know for sure was that Reed had things in his possession that haunted me. She knew broadly what they were. I managed to choke the words out once, then could never muster up the courage to say them out loud again, let alone find the guts to share any details. From that session on, these things were strictly referred to as My Biggest Fear between her and me. All I had to say to her was it triggered My Biggest Fear to come to the surface and she understood what I was referring to. If she ever tried to ask for details or press any further, I practically plugged my ears and yelled.

I looked back at my therapist with heavy eyes and asked, "Was I a mess when I was with him?"

"You were struggling, there is no doubt about that. You really couldn't see anything else happening around you, especially when he disappeared. It would completely engulf you."

I sighed. "I don't even know who I am anymore."

These conversations were all I could think of as I watched Dr. Christine Blasey Ford speak with pure courage during the Brett Kavanaugh confirmation hearings.

Dr. Ford was poised, intelligent, and articulate. The strength in her message hit me right in the heart, as prosecutor Rachel Mitchell tried to poke holes in Dr. Ford's story, implying she was misremembering, even when she *had* opened up about the assault to her husband and therapist. I thought about my own story and how, at a certain point, there would have been next to no evidence. No conversations with friends, no therapist notes, no photos of bruises. Would anyone have believed me if not for the security footage?

I began to fantasize about being called to court to testify against him. I thought if he committed these same crimes again, the law may rain down harder on him. I imagined walking into the courtroom and seeing his face after years had passed. Maybe by then he'd have salt and pepper in his hair and wrinkles by his eyes. I know if this ever happened, Reed would never look up at me. I know if I addressed him, he'd do nothing but stare cowardly down at the floor. He could never face himself.

Dr. Ford opened my eyes even wider to the treatment women receive when they speak up and share their stories of abuse or assault. She is a very credible person to have been sitting in front of the United States Senate Committee on the Judiciary that day. Yet, Republicans tried to discredit every detail she provided about an incident she's had to live with every second of every day since the moment it happened. They tried to discredit her claims about an event that has haunted her and forever-plagued her. Every traumatic sound and smell from that night was seared into her memory. The long term stress it must have caused her. They practically shrugged it all off.

Whether you're sharing with the world like Dr. Ford or sharing with friends like I was, it is risky and often painful. I've rarely felt satisfied by reactions to my story, and the same goes for the world's collective reactions to others.

I have to think it's because the enormity of my feelings will never be matched by anyone. And that has to be okay.

Whatever the scale, you know your experience.

I miss being loved.

CHAPTER 28

Back when Brett and I were still unofficially seeing each other, my little sister and her best friend, Keira, told me one day over lunch that they knew exactly who I should be dating.

"We both think you're destined to be together," Keira told me, eyes sparkling.

I laughed, "Really? Why?"

"Well, he has a dog. An Australian Shepherd named Addy," my sister said.

"Okay," I waited. "Is that the only reason?"

"He's a doctor!" Keira beamed. "And I just think you're, like, perfect for each other! You'd be so cute together!"

"A *doctor*? How old is he?"

"Well, he's studying neuroscience," Keira qualified.

So, I said what any millennial would say, "Let me see his Instagram."

Keira opened his profile and handed me her phone. His name was Michael. I gathered two things right away: He loved his dog, and he dressed impeccably.

My sister and Keira, who I'd grown up with, were both *sure* Michael and I had to meet. Fast forward to soon after Brett and I broke up. My sister and I were seeing an apartment in the west end of the city, and that same night, Keira's boyfriend was having a birthday party a few blocks from the apartment viewing.

"Wanna stop by Jeffrey's birthday with me after?" My sister asked, her voice echoed as we walked around the main floor of an empty High Park home.

"I don't know." I examined the closet space.

"No pressure. It might be fun though. Since we're literally around the corner, I feel like I should at least stop by. You don't have to come, obviously."

I paused then said, "Okay, I'll go if it's just for a bit."

When we arrived through the back door, the first person I saw was the very person whose Instagram they showed me months before. Michael.

Every inch of Michael's outfit was perfectly placed: jeans rolled up tightly, a crisp, perfectly fitted T-shirt, his hair meticulously parted and swept back in just the right way.

He shook my hand with an endearing smile, "Hi, I'm Michael."

"Hi, Michael, I'm Callie."

It was instantly obvious he was kind and respectful. He was a bit shy, very sweet, and throughout the night, it became clear he was kind of the odd one out in his friend group. I liked that. We spent the night getting to know each other. Turned out, we'd grown up just minutes apart in High Park, with lots of friends in common — he'd even been to the apartment I shared with my sister — but somehow, we'd never met.

He wasn't playing hard to get, he wasn't flirting with other girls, he wasn't pretending he wasn't interested.

After a couple of hours in our own little world, the crowd began making plans to leave for the bar. I was in the washroom as everyone piled into the cabs out front. When I stepped out of the washroom, Michael was alone in the empty kitchen, waiting for me.

"Are you coming to the bar?" He asked.

"No, no. I have to go home, I'm exhausted." The truth was, my sister wasn't going and I wasn't about to go out with her friends without her.

I gave Michael a hug, and he said he hoped to see me soon.

As soon as I got home, I followed him on Instagram (ah, romance). The next afternoon, he invited me out for drinks, and later that week we sat on the patio at a small brewery on a sunny afternoon. We talked for hours, and for some unfounded reason, I felt safe.

The first time Michael came to my house for a drink on the balcony, I immediately took off my makeup. I've always struggled with my skin, so much so that even on cottage weekends with girlfriends I would wear concealer (at the very least). But that night, for whatever reason, I had the innate sense Michael wouldn't care that my cheeks were peppered with acne scars.

Being alone with a man was still triggering. Although it wasn't always a conscious fear that they'd be violent, a knot would instantly form in my stomach as waves of guilt crashed over me. I imagine it was self-protection, my own body making the experience so physically uncomfortable that I would make it end. But with Michael, inexplicably, I didn't have that familiar rock sitting deep in my stomach. I wasn't worried that now he knew my address and unit number. I felt like I already knew the sound of his voice and the way he pushed his hair back.

Only a few weeks after our first date, Michael said, "Callie Rae O'Reilly, will you be my girlfriend?"

I really do just want to be happy.

I have to stop worrying.

I can handle things on my own.

CHAPTER 29

So thankful for this creative, kind, wonderful man. The most wonderful human.

These are the words I found on social media written about my abusive ex-boyfriend.

Seven years had passed since I looked him up online — a streak I was proud of. It was good for my mental health. Throughout the first few years after leaving Reed, I had to actively resist searching his name. I had a nagging desire to see his face. *What does his hair look like? Where is he living? Is he still with his girlfriend? Does it seem like he really loves her?* But soon, the desire to know faded and the thought of seeing his face was so painful that I had no urges to fight. Stumbling across Reed on social media would be a nightmare. What could be worse than mindlessly scrolling through snapshots of Italian vacations and an acquaintance's bachelorette party only to be blindsided by your abuser's eyes? I went to far lengths to make sure he never made an unexpected appearance;

I had Marley log into my account to block him, I blocked our friends in common, and I blocked his family.

Things in my life were going well. Michael and I had been together for a few years, and I'd left my job directing to start my own business in the podcasting world. But I was still experiencing panic attacks in the middle of the night. I would lie awake, every cell consumed by someone I once loved becoming a threat to my safety, quality of life, and current relationship. I couldn't take back my mistakes, no matter how much I hated myself. Then, as soon as the sun came up and I was brought back into the reality of life — coffee, emails, groceries — those memories would feel far away and even slightly alarmist once again.

But things evolved.

Soon, graphic flashbacks began to swarm every happy moment: on the boat at my parents' cottage, tucked under a blanket with Michael, walking around the East Village on a weekend away visiting Claire. My brightest moments were suddenly hijacked by vivid, aggressive reminders relentlessly poking at me, reminding me that at one point, life was almost unbearable. They didn't feel like reminders created by my own memory, they felt foreign and sinister, like they'd somehow broken through the gates and were running free, destroying every good thought in their path. With each flashback, my mood would plummet and a veil would be drawn, reminding me not to get too comfortable with being happy. Reed was still out there, those things still happened, and no matter how much therapy I did, no matter how many walks I took or new clothes I bought, nothing could change what existed in my mind. The memories repeatedly pulled me underwater, but I was kicking as hard as I could. So, for the first time in over a decade, I decided to seek out a new therapist, this time, someone specifically trauma focused.

My first trauma therapist, Jackie, had me fill out long questionnaires one Saturday morning in a small room with a tiny desk and an iPad. I settled in with a Starbucks matcha latte to answer questions about the most broken parts of my mind. Jackie then analyzed me over a few long sessions. Eventually, she told me I showed signs of CPTSD. As I learned, the C stands for complex. I'd never heard of this before. She explained that one of the differentiating factors that can lead to CPTSD — rather than PTSD — is repeated exposure to traumatic events. PTSD (post-traumatic stress disorder) often occurs after a one-time event like experiencing a car accident or a natural disaster. CPTSD occurs in people who have been in abusive relationships, experienced childhood neglect, or lived through a war, for example. It is because of events that spanned over a period of time.

I felt like a fraud comparing what I'd been through to someone who'd experienced childhood neglect. My life had otherwise been a breeze — privileged, protected, and easy. Comparing real struggle to the consequences of one person I met at eighteen seemed ignorant. But my therapist told me repeated exposure to that type of toxic behaviour created new neural pathways in my brain. It pulled that now familiar veil down over my eyes and caused me to see the whole world a couple shades darker. As time passed, I got so used to that lens that eventually I could no longer notice a difference.

I continued to see Jackie for a few months. But after each session, I was left with a bit of dread bubbling low. Something about her approach with me wasn't meshing as I'd hoped.

Jackie felt strongly about a treatment where I'd take Propranolol — a beta blocker — before our session, then talk through the trauma. The medication would block my adrenaline and help me to talk in much more detail, allowing me to process the trauma, then store it as any other memory. She had successfully used this form of therapy with previous clients and saw great improvement. I understood there were perfectly legitimate forms of therapy out there which simply weren't up my alley and taking medication before a session was one of them.

I told her, "I just don't think that's *me*. I don't even like to take Advil some days. It all just makes me a bit anxious." If she had let it go the first time I tried to politely side-step the suggestion,

I would probably have stuck with Jackie because I liked her. I felt safe and knew she cared. But Jackie continued to bring it up each session, urging me to try the Propranolol treatment, leaving me feeling pressured. Eventually she wore me down so much that I called my doctor for the Propranolol prescription, which he gave me. My doctor also assured me the medication was safe. He said he prescribes it to patients who have a fear of public speaking before major events at work, for example. I believed both him and Jackie. But still, it wasn't something I was interested in, and I felt as though Jackie saw it as my only way forward.

Jackie was also quick to attribute all my thoughts to trauma. Michael and I moved into an apartment above a paper store right on Toronto's trendy Queen Street West, directly across the street from one of the city's busiest parks, Trinity Bellwoods. The building had a fire escape up the back and felt like a baby New York. At first, it seemed perfect, close to cafés, restaurants, parks, away from the stale grind of the downtown core. But we could hear every step the neighbours above us took. It drove me so crazy that I felt like I was going to burst into tears or smash my windows. I couldn't take it. I felt like the walls were closing in, like I had no space of my own, always sitting, waiting, listening for the next sound. When I called Jackie and told her what was happening, expressing concern for myself and my over-the-top reaction, she told me, "Callie, this is a trauma response."

Confused and skeptical, I asked, "A trauma response? How?"

She told me, "Your space feels violated. It may be triggering something inside of you that's making you feel unsafe. I would bet that your reaction is directly related to your trauma. You feel unsafe and exposed at the hands of someone else."

At the time, I thought this was yet another reason I should stop seeing Jackie and find someone who "got me." It seemed far-fetched. Not everything in my life was about Reed and the abuse. I was just annoyed and wished the neighbours would quit staying up quite so late. But now, I think she may have had a point. Those feelings of anxiety, believing like I had nowhere safe to go, nowhere comfortable — they're the exact feelings I had back then. Immediately, I'm transported to the time when I wasn't safe at Reed's but couldn't go home and face Marley. I had no space of my own, no home where I felt safe, and nowhere to relax my nervous system.

Still, I decided to stop seeing Jackie.

My second trauma therapist-turned-lifesaver, Paul, explained that in order to see any real progress with the trauma, I eventually needed to address my worst memory, which he described as being at the top of the pyramid. It didn't have to be the most violent or scary, just the memory that, for whatever reason, ranked highest in my mind. If I didn't reach to the top and then work my way down, I wouldn't tackle the trauma in its entirety.

This was easy to identify but difficult to speak out loud. At that point, I'd never shared the true details with anyone — not friends, not family, barely even the therapist I'd been seeing since I was eighteen. But there was still that one recurring thought I couldn't shake. The one that crept out from under my bed in the middle of the night. One thought that gave me a physical reaction to any reminder and left me feeling closely tethered to Reed for life. Because of this one memory, no matter how much my life moved on, I felt as though he was able to assault me whenever he felt like it.

That thought was knowing Reed could potentially still see me graphically naked. When my therapist and I talk about that tip of the pyramid, I realized this was the summit where Reed planted his flag. I believed if Michael knew about my sexual history with Reed, he would leave me.

Eventually, I found myself in the appointment Paul had warned me about weeks earlier. I showed up with two stories; the first was the most damaging on paper. The one that sounded worst to the ear, but in reality, wasn't what haunted me repeatedly. The other was the truth, my most painful and humiliating. The one I could barely manage to acknowledge to myself, let alone speak out loud, especially to a man. I told Paul I brought two because they were both the worst — equally — but I was lying.

I got through the first story mater-of-fact. I could deliver it almost entirely on autopilot. *I tried to open the front door, but he wouldn't let me out. Then he picked me up and threw me backwards onto the bed. I managed to get up, but he threw me backwards again.* I was proud of how I believed I was coming across to my therapist: strong, brave, over it. When I finished, he simply asked to hear the second story. I sensed a shift inside of me, as if my nerves had just braced for impact. My hands began to shake as I scrolled down. Butterflies awoke in my stomach. Nausea rolled and swayed. I'd never had this physical reaction, then again, I'd never told anyone this story out loud in great detail without hiding the most shameful parts.

A few months after we got back together, we decided to film ourselves having sex. I think it was my idea. I spoke softly, as if keeping quiet made my choices less true. I read quickly, fast-forwarding over the most damning words. *After I asked him to delete it, he brought his laptop with him each time he left the house. He asked me if I would leave him if he deleted it.*

Halfway into reading it aloud, I started to cry. It's rare that I cry when talking about this time in my life, but this day was different. I wasn't consumed by anxiety like I was that night in Cat's bed. This time, I was really listening to the words I was saying. And for the first time, I felt a little bit sad for myself. I was sad I had to work through these things, sad I felt so embarrassed. I was exhausted from still carrying such immense shame, ashamed that I hadn't been courageous enough to really open up to anyone closest to me.

As the words went from paper to voice, I let myself float outside of my own body. Without that separation, the shame would have been crushing.

When I finished, Paul was quiet for a moment, sighed deeply, then said, "I'm so sorry these things happened. I'm sorry you're carrying so much shame about it. And thank you for telling me. I can see how difficult it is for you."

I heard his words, I saw his kind eyes looking back at me, I knew he meant what he was saying.

Paul went on, "I just don't see the video as a mistake. It's something a lot of people do. A lot. I wouldn't call it a mistake." I almost couldn't process his words. I'd barely ever spoken any of it out loud before, so I'd never given anyone the chance to help release me. But by saying that, Paul was releasing me. He's a dad. He's smart, compassionate, and educated. He was listening to my most shameful experiences, my ugliest most inner thoughts, my most humiliating choices. He was hearing me. By telling me that, in his eyes, he didn't see it as a mistake, he was setting me free and opening the door — ever so slightly — for me to start forgiving myself. "You don't think it was a mistake? How?" I needed to hear the words. "I think it was an insurmountable mistake. What if he posts it somewhere? Sometimes the thought makes me want to die. Michael would leave me if he knew."

"First of all, give Michael a bit more credit. And second, you did something with someone you trusted at the time, with the knowledge you had at that time." Paul said.

"I think that's letting myself off the hook too easily. I knew the type of person he was. There were little things. Sure, the worst of the abuse hadn't happened, but some smaller things had." I couldn't excuse my choices quite so easily.

"Okay, but, you didn't have *all* of the information you have now. You didn't know what you know now, so you can't look at it through your eyes today. You did what you wanted to do with your boyfriend when you were so young." He pushed back. "Doing it wasn't wrong. What was wrong was the abuse. Don't forget that."

It was a thought that seemed almost ludicrous.

My healthy mind is capable of accepting that the things we did weren't wrong. Having a sexual relationship with my long-term boyfriend wasn't wrong. Even filming ourselves having sex wasn't wrong — it was a choice I made with my partner at a time when

I was in love, happy, and that part of my life was just starting to take shape. Unfortunately, it's laced with a layer of shame — as sex almost always comes with shame in the eyes of society if you're a woman — and on top of that, my relationship with Reed was already soaked in it. But, I only knew what I knew.

The painful memories of my sexual experiences with Reed plagued my relationship with my body and with sex, and it was at this point they became impossible to control. Most of what made that relationship toxic manifested itself onto my physical self. It felt as though everything traumatic used my body as its conduit, and I can't run away from that body. I'm unable to escape the vessel, forever with the scars and memories of what he did to it, forever feeling a little bit used and a little bit gross. Knowing there's a chance he can look at my body whenever he wants leaves me feeling repeatedly assaulted. It's a thought that, in my darkest moments, has left me suicidal.

Paul helped me make sense of it like this: If someone is sexually assaulted on the subway, they may be too triggered to ever ride the subway again. They may avoid public transit altogether, for years or even the rest of their life. For me, that subway is my body, with no option to avoid it. Instead of avoidance, I have to find ways to cope with learned tools to tolerate the distress.

The possibility of Reed still having a tangible piece of my physical being is something I must learn to live with and forgive myself for. There is no way around it other than pressing forward, headfirst into the thoughts, and finding ways to manage. Nothing I can do will change the reality. I cannot erase the choices I made, so I have to learn how to live with them, starting with addressing self-blame.

By 2017, ten years since its release, Kim Kardashian's sex tape had amased 210 million views. A staggering number. Kim Kardashian is a woman who prides herself on being able to do it all; she can have a meeting at the White House one day and pose for her shapewear brand, Skims, the next. She is powerful, successful, and continuously shamed for being sexual, the very thing that propels her success.

She's a woman I've thought of when my darkest thoughts about my own "sex tape" chase me down the narrow hallways of my sweatiest nightmares. She is polarizing; some people still believe she isn't allowed to be sexual if she wants to be taken seriously. And yet, her sex tape has hundreds of millions of views. So which is it: In the eyes of the world, is it shameful and wrong, or sexy and intriguing? I suppose the answer lies in each person's individual relationship to their own shame.

It's easy to shake our fingers and judge a woman for being sexual, for posing nearly naked on Instagram, or agreeing to being filmed. (To quote Joey Tribbiani, "If a girl says yes to being taped, she doesn't say no to much else.") But a lot of those doing the shaming, I'd bet, have felt the same wrath, or have watched Kim Kardashian's sex tape. Who should we really be ashamed of? And where is the shame pointed at her then-partner, Ray J?

After working through my shame with Paul, I eventually found moments of freedom. Everyone has a body, and it wasn't my fault he chose to weaponize my own against me. That would be his karma to live with, not mine. Then there are the other days. The other days when I'm still mentally tortured by the thought, crying in the shower, planning how I'll explain it to my family, and figuring out what I'll do when my life falls apart. My stomach twists at the thought of Reed looking at my naked body. I picture him sitting in the apartment I knew so well, bare feet flat on the ground, opening the file we promised to delete, my body frozen in time, depressed and abused.

He may still have a part of my most hurting self behind lock and key, and I can't change that. I can never get that part of myself back. I save my money with this specific fear in mind; I'll need it when I lose everyone and everything. I lay awake in the night, haunted, trying to decide who would turn their back on me. Who would I lose? Who would I still have? Do I even deserve to have anyone?

Some nights, I squeeze my eyes shut and will myself back to age sixteen, back to my first kiss when it was enough to provide happiness until the end of time. If I think hard enough about the person I was before I made these mistakes, maybe I'll wake up and be her again. Maybe if I remind myself of the smallest details, like the feeling of getting to school in the morning when the weather was just starting to get cold, or the way my parents' house smelled, or my high school uniform, I'll wake up sixteen and none of this will have happened. Maybe I can be happy if I just focus hard enough.

These bad days left me feeling disgusted and betrayed by my own body, unable to look at myself without thinking of the mistakes I made with it. Getting out of the shower, I'd make sure to cover myself with a towel before accidentally seeing myself reflected back in the foggy mirror. I didn't want to see my body move, imagining it as a glimpse into what he has seen, too. Every arch of my back, lift of my leg, that's how he knows my body. And there was a time when I hated it. I gave myself away like I meant nothing to me.

As Paul helped me forgive myself, I began to realize my experiences have power. There is a reason to share them, even only for myself. They aren't just stories that I can feel falsely proud of speaking about out loud about without my eyes getting watery. They are things that happened, mistakes I've had to think about, choices I've had to live with. There was abuse that warranted therapy. I was hesitant to talk about it because of the time in my life that it happened. I was in my late teens and early twenties. Does it really matter what happened if it all took place while I was so young? Is there a sliding scale of impact relative to age? There are women who experience abuse for decades at the hands of their husbands. They have kids. They go through their entire lives full of fear. They're financially controlled. Compared to those women, do my experiences even matter? I was a baby.

But as I finally said my worst memories out loud, I realized my stories do have meaning. Because every abusive relationship starts with an innocent crush, a nervous first date, an uncomfortable first argument, a confusing first sign of violence, a shaky attempt at leaving, and a horrible relief when going back. There is meaning in how it all unfolded, and there is learning to share. It doesn't matter if it happened when I was sixteen or fifty-six.

I'm still hesitant to share out of fear of saying the wrong thing or something I've said being taken the wrong way. I know I'll have sleepless nights over my most personal stories being read by strangers, and even worse, by people who do know me. I know my entire body is going to turn hot at the thought of strange eyes reading intimate details about my sex life. But that's when I'll try to channel the courage of the women I look up to who have shared their stories, and I'll remind myself how helpful those women were to my own healing. I'll remind myself how their stories helped me when I felt like I was being held underwater. I'll remind myself how they gave me the courage to speak up. How their bravery changed my life. I, too, am nothing but strange eyes reading their most intimate details, but by sharing their thoughtful, brave words, they were bringing me back to life. And that much outweighs everything else. So, when heat starts to crawl up the back of my neck, I'll try to take a deep breath in and out. I'll think of twenty-year-old me and finally give her the grace and patience she deserved, acknowledge the nuance, the pain, and the shame she was too young to understand.

- Don't isolate!
- Be with people who love you
- Listen to music
- Don't beat yourself up
- Sleep
- Make a gratitude list
- Don't lose hope

CHAPTER 30

So thankful for this creative, kind, wonderful man. The most wonderful human.

When I opened Pandora's box of internet stalking Reed again, it became disgustingly apparent that while I was living in fear of him exposing me for having had an intimate relationship — God forbid — he did not live in fear of me exposing him as an abuser. I found a past local photography exhibit and numerous posts showing off his work. He was not hiding like I was. Meanwhile, I was keeping my social media profiles private and not revealing too much about my relationship or career.

But afterwards, as I sat with my newfound knowledge of adult Reed, I curiously started to feel lighter, a feeling I hardly recognized. He didn't seem to be living in fear of what I knew, of the things he'd done. It was me who was scared, me who was ashamed of myself. The backward thinking was abundantly clear: Women having any sort of sexuality is a fate worse than being an abuser in our world. In fact, women having any sort of sexuality is a fate worse than most things in our world.

Learning how to release myself from the false idea that Reed held more power than I did was key to healing. My body is not more shameful than his abuse. It's a realization that filled my stomach with flickers of determination, overriding the usual nausea of self-blame.

Now I see you happy.
Habitual jealousy.
But once longed
For your loyalty
The creases by your eyes
I used to have memorized.
The veins in your hands
And our imaginary plans
I knew you
I wanted to
But you took me apart
Rebuilt me from the start
Leaving the pieces I liked
But you told me it was right.
Now you see me happy.
The way it should be.
An ocean from your toxicity
Wishing to erase me.
And instead
He sees me
Just be.

CHAPTER 31

There is a little two-second moment at the end of my day that makes me smile. I stay up much later than Michael. He's a morning person; he wakes up early and takes his dog for a long walk. Then he works out, has a shower, makes coffee, relaxes. Finally, he starts his work day, all before I'm awake.

I stay up late, writing. Every night, a couple of hours after Michael's fallen asleep, I sneak into our bedroom, rub in some hand lotion, plug in my phone, and turn on the sound machine. Once I finally climb under the covers, and if I've woken him up that night, Michael reaches back and touches my legs. Just for a split second. It happens so quickly and it's so small, I doubt he thinks anything of it. But more often than I'd like to admit, I feel nauseating anxiety creeping in when I see the back of Michael's head on the pillow next to mine. Without actively thinking about it, my body tells me to be careful. He might be angry, don't wake him up. The conditioned part of my brain wonders if he's facing away because he's angry, or worse, ignoring me. My body will suddenly fear this man next to me. But with that gentle nudge as I climb into bed beside him, Michael reminds me that he is safe and I am safe.

"Okay, I think I have it. I think this could work." I told Michael as we walked our dogs around our downtown Toronto neighbourhood.

"Let's hear it," Michael said.

"What if, when we go to London for Christmas, we just . . . stay." I paused, waiting for Michael's logical mind to mull.

It was September. I was suggesting we pack up our lives and move across the world in just two and a half months. After only a short moment, Michael said, "Interesting. That *could* work."

Michael and I — both born and raised Torontonians — had been feeling restless in Toronto for a few years now. My relationship with the city was tarnished years earlier and Michael was growing bored of the views we knew.

Michael had never been to London, in fact, he'd never been to Europe, but I felt strongly he'd love it. Plus, my older sister lived there, and she was expecting her first baby.

"You love New York, and trust me, you'll love London. It's beautiful and *clean*." I'd been making my pitch for a few years, on and off, but only recently did we start seriously considering it.

Sure enough, two and a half months later, Michael and I folded our lives into boxes and shipped ourselves (and one dog, we decided Dex was too old for the flight) across the ocean. I sat looking out the plane window. As the sun was rising, and lush London was only just waking up, I suddenly thought of Reed and how, finally, even just for a year or two, I could leave that pain behind. London and I hardly knew each other. There would be no neighbourhoods to dodge, no streets to avoid. No monsters lurking. It was a giant, rainy, beautiful blank slate that didn't know Reed's name.

Months later, I stood leaning against the outside of a London pub refreshing Twitter. The Amber Heard/Johnny Depp verdict would be revealed any moment.

As I watched the slew of Johnny Depp support rush through social media like the plague, I had trouble understanding the blind eye being turned to the indisputable abuse the trial had unearthed: violent, threatening text messages, destroyed property, and even a video proving his rage. I watched as people I know (and love) supported Depp on Instagram, wondering how they could stand behind someone who, post-wedding to Amber Heard, allegedly told a friend, "We're married — now I can punch her in the face and nobody can do anything about it." Then it hit me: those who have experience with abuse were one step ahead, having already accepted the very thing Depp fans were struggling to accept now. And it's the most bitter of pills to swallow.

Before the trial began, I'll admit, my feelings were complicated. I, too, had *overwhelmingly* seen anti–Amber Heard content in what felt like years leading up to it. My knowledge of Heard came only from her marriage to Johnny Depp, and yet, my knowledge of him spanned decades. This established familiarity with Depp had me unconsciously lean in one direction, while my knee-jerk reaction to believe women pulled me back to the middle.

Wanting to form my own opinions, I began watching the trial, something I also felt was my appointed duty as a woman who has experienced domestic violence.

Eventually, Heard took the stand and began detailing the alleged abuse she experienced at the hands of Depp. Scared for her, I sat quietly and held my breath.

Watching from my small West London apartment became my little way of supporting Amber Heard as she took on forces greater than herself and even greater than Johnny Depp. All victims were watching little pieces of their own stories play out in front of the world. I also figured I should know how these types of trials go: the histories they dredge up, the people they rope in, the humiliation that accompanies a defamation trial like this one, no matter what the scale. We women need to know.

Amber Heard hadn't even named Johnny Depp in the essay at the centre of it all.

Noted.

I forced myself to watch the treatment Heard was receiving, both in the courtroom and through every comment, article, post, and Tweet. It was my way of planting my feet firmly next to hers in the trenches the only way I knew how. She is a fellow woman. An abused woman. And a woman going up against one of the most powerful, beloved, established men in Hollywood. Heard was mocked online for wearing glasses, for smiling, for not smiling, for the clothes she wore, for the way she did her hair, for hugging her legal team, for not hugging her legal team, for rolling her eyes, for smirking, for having no expression at all. Depp, on the other hand, was praised for his snarky comments, for eating candy, and for laughing.

Throughout the trial, Depp presented himself as sweeter and gentler than the average man. He was soft-spoken, shy, docile, abundantly polite and, at times, almost fragile. He carried himself with a certain vulnerability that, juxtaposed with Heard's claims, felt shoe-horned into Depp's unassuming disposition. He addressed his ex-wife exclusively as Ms. Heard, apologized gently when he spoke out of turn, and made sure to always lead with manners, even when his comments were laced with sarcasm. And yet, the next moment, a text message from Depp was read aloud: *Let's drown her before we burn her!!! I will fuck her burnt corpse afterwards to make sure she is dead.* Easy as it may be for some to deny Heard's allegations, there is no denying the violent, abusive nature of texts like these, which came directly from Depp and which were explained away as his dark sense of humour — an excuse I'm tired of hearing. In my eyes, those texts alone are worth never seeing a Johnny Depp film ever again.

And yet, somehow, for a short period of time, even I found myself occasionally sucked into the "Southern gentleman"-ness of Johnny Depp. He was overly respectful; my TikTok algorithm showed thirsty clips of him pulling out the chair for his female lawyer, shaking the hand of every courthouse staff member, and greeting adoring fans who'd waited hours just to catch a glimpse of Captain Jack Sparrow. He was racking up the gentleman points, not the type of man who could possibly have raped Amber Heard with a liquor bottle.

The ability of my hardened shell to be even slightly softened by the familiarity and politeness of this actor I grew up with was surprising even to me. Surprising because my abuser, too, was polite, shy, and quiet. He could appear gentle and even vulnerable. Endearingly awkward and reserved. Seemingly incapable of allowing his eyes to fill with rage or throwing me around his apartment when I tried to leave him. Casually observing my ex-partner from a distance wouldn't necessarily sound alarms of his anger lying dormant just beneath the surface. Without knowing who he was behind closed doors, one would look at his calm mannerisms — and manners — and not necessarily assume he was a threat to women in his orbit. Odd and complicated, sure, but violent may be a stretch. He was passive and moved through the world at a relatively low decibel.

But oftentimes, people are not entirely as they seem. And those complexities are impossible to gather through press junkets, late-night interviews, and sometimes, even after months of sleeping next to them. The forceful, unwavering certainty of the public that Johnny Depp is a kind, calm, generous man — and nothing else — simply because he's been on movie screens and appears kind in front of a camera swayed almost every corner of the internet, leaving no room for complexity of character, or the possibility there could be another side to Depp — one that exists only behind padlocked doors, shielded from the wide eyes of his fans.

Like it or not, Depp sent those texts joking about killing Amber Heard.

It may take time to accept the person you thought you knew, the actor you believed in, the man you've looked up to may not be who you thought. This is precisely what Amber Heard — and all victims — have had to accept when it comes to their abusers: The person they love isn't who they'd hoped.

That is to say, I know how difficult this is. Accepting that someone you've revered can be violent, controlling, and angry, requires mental acrobatics. Accepting that someone you've chosen to share a bed with is abusive — even harder. But this recalibration cannot come at the expense of the victim's experiences and credibility. These things take time. It is possible and reasonable to mourn the loss of who you believed Johnny Depp was, while also supporting Amber Heard as a victim (even if she isn't the "perfect victim," whatever that means). As with everything, two things can be true at the same time, and we must learn how to make room for this, especially in circumstances like these. I, for one, would much rather stand with the woman in this situation, and be proved wrong, than deny the funny, jokey texts about fucking his wife's dead body.

As I stood outside that pub in Central London, the verdict was announced.

My stomach dropped. She lost.

My heart broke as if it had been my own relationship on trial. The pub smelled of beer and cigarette smoke, and I watched groups of men in suits laughing, tourists shopping, red buses passing.

Meanwhile, Depp was celebrating his win at a pub not too far away.

The Depp/Heard verdict exposed all victims' worst fears: Speaking up — even without naming your abuser — may land you humiliated and belittled, possibly never able to work again, with faceless voyeurs labelling you a "lying bitch," or, as Heard herself shared, having strangers threaten to microwave her one-year-old child.

Of course, this trial between two beautiful, successful celebrities was scrutinized for its level of coverage when there are other tragedies happening around the world. A point I do take and understand. But we must not dismiss the effect this particular trial and its subsequent social commentary has had on victims around the world. It is a vessel for fear to be further pumped into the veins of those who are in the process of rebuilding their lives or those who have just found the courage to leave a violent relationship, or worse, those about to enter the courtroom to face their newly emboldened abuser (not to mention Evan Rachel Wood and FKA Twigs, two women who faced two other famous men).

Then came Danny Masterson. The actor who played band-T-wearing, pot-smoking, sunglasses-donning, sarcastic Steven Hyde on *That '70s Show*, found guilty of raping two women in the early 2000s, the height of his fame. It was a tough pill to swallow for those around my age with a soft spot for the show. I remained slightly removed from the Masterson trial, protecting my delicate hopes that were obliterated post Depp/Heard. But my ears perked up once again when it came the time for sentencing. I went in with minimal hope, expecting, yet again, a famous white man to walk away with little to no punishment for the violent crimes he committed against women.

This time, something different happened. The disappointment came later, after the successful thirty-to-life sentence, when letters to the judge from fellow *That '70s Show* co-stars (and real-life married couple) Ashton Kutcher ("Michael Kelso") and Mila Kunis ("Jackie Burkhart") leaked to the public, asking for leniency in his sentencing.

Now, they're also just celebrities who act. Assigning too much weight to their opinions would be, to an extent, irresponsible. However, I had a little bit of faith in Kutcher in particular, because of his work with Thorn, an anti-child-trafficking organization he co-founded in 2012.

But shortly after Danny Masterson's sentencing, a rumour whispered through the internet that Ashton Kutcher had written a post-verdict character statement on behalf of Masterson. And shortly after that, both Kutcher and Kunis's letters were leaked to the public. In his letter, Kutcher writes that Danny Masterson is his friend, co-worker, and role model of twenty-five years. Kutcher describes Masterson as honest, decent, generous, a hands-on dad to his daughter and a loyal husband. Kutcher ends the letter with:

> *While I'm aware that the judgement has been cast as guilty on two counts of rape by force and the victims have a great desire for justice. I hope that my testament to his character is taken into consideration in sentencing. I do not believe he is an ongoing harm to society and having his daughter raised without a present father would* [be] *a tertiary injustice in and of itself. Thank you for taking the time to read this.*

Because Ashton Kutcher was not one of Danny Masterson's victims, I can see a world where Kutcher believes every word of this to be the truth. His truth. And it's a direct reflection of the cunning duality that lies within those who commit violent acts toward women. They can be all these things: generous, dedicated, courteous, kind, and also, a rapist.

The world is just now catching up to what Danny Masterson's victims have known since the early 2000s: sometimes, those you love, those who you once trusted to be around your daughter, those who acted as a mentor are different people behind closed doors.

The Depp/Heard trial was a trial between rich, white celebrities, but the repercussions were felt by everyday victims in very real ways. Victims whose social media feeds were filled with Johnny Depp support from those closest to them, people who previously may have felt non-threatening. I will always remember who those people were on my own feed, including those who liked Depp's celebratory post. But let's not forget, victims are simply one step ahead. They've already come to terms with the very thing Johnny Depp fans and friends of Danny Masterson are only now struggling with: Sometimes, in the end, those you have loved are not what they seemed. Heartbreaking, isn't it?

Michael put down his empty Guinness glass, wrapped an arm around my shoulder, and squeezed me gently. "I'm so sorry," he said, after the Depp/Heard verdict. "I know what this means to you. Let's go home."

We caught the District Underground line back to Chiswick. As London flew by the windows, I played with a sapphire ring on my finger. Michael and I were engaged. He proposed on a little Twickenham cobblestone street full of twinkle lights and cozy shops, and we spent our first night as an engaged couple with my sisters, their husbands, and my brand-new nephew, safe and at peace.

LIVING

I didn't realize what he was doing.

CHAPTER 32

It was a warm evening at my parents' cottage. The sun was just going down, casting an orange haze over the lake. It was one of those perfect nights when the world stands still and worries feel far away. The smell of barbecue wafted through the air and the distant hum of boats echoed across the lake. We ate dinner on the porch: corn on the cob, burgers, baked potatoes, and an enormous Caesar salad. On nights like these, we always take a vote: Who wants to go for a boat ride? Who wants to have a fire? Who wants dessert first?

We chose a boat ride. Leaving the dishes in the sink for later, we threw on our sandals, grabbed soft sweaters, and made our way down the rocky path to the dock. As I got closer to the lake, I could smell the water. The smell of summer. We piled in — my parents, Michael, my sisters, my brothers-in-law, my nephew, and my dogs. My dad started the boat — a sound that has always reminded me of being a little kid, terrified of spiders hiding in the crooks of my lifejacket.

I sat at the front, holding on to Dex. He propped himself up onto the edge of the boat and put his curious little nose up into the wind. There's a lot to smell for little dogs like Dex. I peered into each cottage as we drifted by. It seemed everyone was up that weekend. Some were still floating on noodles, while others were wrapped in plush towels on the dock. They waved as we passed.

Perfect evenings like these used to make me ache with sadness. Sadness from knowing there was a time when I felt like the world was a dark place, one I wasn't sure I wanted to remain a part of. Sadness that there was a time when I doubted there were good people. Now, looking across the still lake at the tangerine sun, I was heartbroken at the thought of ever feeling trapped with someone who had made me feel so small, someone who spat on me and slapped me, when there were people who really loved me.

There is so much good in my little world. There are so many reasons not to give up and surrender to the poison I felt had been tattooed onto the fabric of who I was. There are summer evenings, nights on the dock watching the stars, hours of laughing around the dining room table. There are birthdays, weddings, and anniversaries to celebrate. There are family trips, long walks with Dex and Addy, and tasty pasta. There are sad movies and great books. Hampstead Heath and Chiswick House. There are nights in bed with hot chocolate and *Friends* reruns. There are pumpkins to carve, pancakes to make, and iced matcha lattes to drink. Christmas Eves and Christmas mornings. First snows and spring rain. There are concerts, new albums, Taylor Swift Easter eggs. There are Sunday mornings, fall air, and warm bubble baths.

There is joy.

For a couple years, everything went black. I would walk down the street examining each person who passed by, wondering if they wanted to die like I did. I wondered if they could tell by my sunken eyes and wobbly knees that I was barely hanging on, contemplating not doing it anymore. There were days I wondered if I would ever feel unburdened again or if that version of me had died. I wondered if the person I used to be was launched out of my insides when I was thrown against the wall.

But now I know there is more good in the world than one mimic is capable of stealing. He was a scared boy whose body seemed to grow without him.

Instead, my dad answers the phone with, "Hi, Honey!" My mom with, "Hi, Peanut!" And I know I am loved.

I've forgiven myself for being unable to see it for a few years. Life was heavy and I thought no one could understand. I've forgiven myself for losing my way and, for a brief moment, not really wanting to find my way back. I've forgiven myself for slipping into a world that wasn't mine with someone who wasn't mine. That time gave me the gift of perspective and the strength to fight for myself — the strength to never go back. Because witnessing everything life has to offer makes it all worth it. Michael, my dad, my mom, my sisters, my niece and nephew, they are worth it.

If you are waking up with bruises, or have ever felt trapped, you will find the good again. Because it shouldn't hurt, and it won't always hurt. Remember summer evenings, remember the perfect song playing in the car, and remember laughing with the people who love you most. That goodness is still there. Don't give up on it.

A friend of mine read an early version of these chapters and suggested I answer one question: *How do you feel knowing Reed may read it*? I thought I was having trouble articulating a response until I realized the answer is clear: I feel nothing.

When I look at old photos, I feel divided from my body. Distant. My tattoos were so fresh. So thin. Now they bleed, smudge and move. Ten years older. Ten years of life experience. The me you knew is gone. The anger has resolved. I've slowly rebuilt myself.

CHAPTER 33

On a sunny, unseasonably warm December afternoon, our house was full of noise, busy and bustling with makeup stations and champagne flutes. The boys sat downstairs in the living room listening to music and laughing. Upstairs in our bedroom, I slid into a black dress with strings of pearls hanging from the waist, put on chunky silver heels, checked my ponytail one last time, and touched up my poppy red Glossier lip stain.

"Here, let me fix one thing," Michael's sister said. I bent down to meet her. She gently adjusted my hair as her one-year-old son crawled around our feet, reaching for the pearls swaying from my dress. "Gentle!" She softly reminded him.

Just a few minutes later, Michael and I were married next to twinkling Christmas lights. We decided not to have a traditional wedding, both too shy for an audience. Instead, we signed papers at our brick farmhouse in the country with just four witnesses and no vows spoken.

I grappled with this milestone for more reasons than one. I worried we would become two people who once loved each other. I feared losing myself to the joint identity of a couple. But mostly, I worried I would never be ready to fuse my life to another person. I was scared to lose not just a relationship but a home and life if we fell apart. It was obvious where these fears were born.

But Michael is gentle, frustratingly intelligent, and unparalleled in his thoughtfulness. He cooks only meals that I like, not the food he actually prefers. He's never annoyed when I can't find my keys as we're rushing out the door. He looks at me every time we pass a cute dog, just to make sure I saw it, too. He will always take the middle seat. When I'm having an anxious day, he heats up the hot water bottle and lifts our dogs onto the bed. And when I told him I wanted to move to London, he packed his bags to fulfill that dream.

Michael and I got married just after our seven-year anniversary. By then, the vividness of my past experiences had mostly dulled. Or maybe they just didn't scare me as much anymore. I'd spent hours in therapy, days alone processing, hours writing. No longer did the harshest flashes of violence replay in my mind, whipping through my calmest days. I'd released the memories, finally believing they are no longer my burdens to carry and never were.

But lingering still was the instinct to run away from someone capable of rattling my foundation. Lurking still was the fear of allowing a relationship to take centre stage in my life, dictating my days, my happiness, my future. It was the possibility of those things being stolen — my safety, my steadiness — which left scars too deep to fade. Losing myself the way I had was the scariest thing of all, because that blame wasn't quite as easy to assign.

This isn't what I would have guessed would linger.

But it was losing myself that was most damaging, the feeling of free-falling alone, because it shattered any ideas of what my world could become.

Now, I can trust myself enough to know that I would get through it, and certain things are worth such a scary jump.

Having a steady, loving husband is not the answer to these lasting questions. It isn't a good man doing the healing for me or the Disney end to my story — I don't want one — because I will never define my life in those terms. Instead, my career, my happiness, and my marriage are evidence of self-forgiveness and sturdy independence. Without making peace with myself and having faith in myself, those other pieces of my life would not be possible. The passing of time has allowed me to accept and move forward, and in that, I'm left with a braver and wiser version of myself, always there, in case I need her. And maybe that's my happy ending.

The End

ACKNOWLEDGEMENTS

This book would not exist if it weren't for my brilliant agent, Claire Cavanagh. Thank you, Claire, for seeing something in this book and in me as a writer. Because of you, I was able to transform this experience into something entirely new. Thank you for leading me through with kindness, encouragement and lightness. You make it so fun.

My editor, Pia Singhal. Thank you, Pia, for taking a chance on me and this debut memoir. Thank you for making it the warmest, safest place to write, and for such thoughtful, insightful notes and conversations. I am endlessly grateful.

To my publisher, ECW. Thank you to the entire team. From the beautiful artwork design to the production coordination and copyedit, I appreciate every single one of you and the work you put into this book. Thank you for making me look better than I am.

To the friends who saved my life. Marley, B, Laine, Claire. And those who brought me back to life all these years later. I'll never forget it. You supported me even when this seemed like an impossible goal. Thank you for reading early versions and for reminiscing (even about the bad times) as I worked to connect the dots.

Dad. Thank you for showing me the possibility in creativity. Thank you for teaching me that everything is possible, no matter what. I wouldn't know myself without you. Our safest place, the net that always appears. I have moulded myself after you.

Mom. Our guide, our comfort, our everything. Thank you for carrying it alongside me when it was too heavy to carry alone. You are safety, you are strength, you are joy. Thank you for always answering my texts in the middle of the night.

Big Sister. Thank you for always welcoming your little sisters into your world. The most fun with the best laugh. Thank you for sharing the absolute joy of your little ones with me every single day.

Little Sister. Thank you for lending me some of your brilliance when I felt like I couldn't write this book. Thank you for believing in me, always, no matter what. Thank you for making me laugh and for reading my mind. I'm happiest with you.

And to my Michael. Thank you for your gentle understanding while, for five years, I spent every evening and weekend writing. Thank you for taking me out to celebrate each step of the publishing journey. You changed everything. You are home.